Michael A. Vigil

THE PRIMACY OF PETER

THE PRIMACY OF PETER

Essays in Ecclesiology and the Early Church

Edited by

John Meyendorff

ST VLADIMIR'S SEMINARY PRESS
CRESTWOOD, NEW YORK
1992

Library of Congress Cataloging-in-Publication Data

The Primacy of Peter: essays in ecclesiology and the early church / by John
  Meyendorff ... [et al.].
  p.   cm.
Includes index.
ISBN 0–88141–125–6
1. Peter the Apostle, Saint. 2. Popes—Primacy. 3. Orthodox Eastern
Church—Doctrines. I. Meyendorff, John, 1926–   .
BS2515.P675   1992
262'.13—dc20   92–6455
                                                               CIP

THE PRIMACY OF PETER
THIS EDITION COPYRIGHT © 1992
by

ST VLADIMIR'S SEMINARY PRESS

ISBN 0–88141–125–6

First published in English by The Faith Press, Ltd. in 1963.
Parts of this edition translated from the French edition,
Delachaux et Niestle, Neuchâtel and Paris.

PRINTED IN THE UNITED STATES OF AMERICA

Contents

Essays 4 and 5 translated by Katharine Farrer

Introduction

Published originally in English almost three decades ago (1963), the present collection of studies is being reprinted—with the addition of a new article by Veselin Kesich—to meet the needs of a continuing ecclesiological debate. The articles of Nicholas Afanasieff and Alexander Schmemann could not be bibliographically updated, because the authors are deceased.

All the articles touch upon the issue which originated the *fundamental* and scandalous divisions in Christendom: the schism between East and West. Historians have shown that the exact date of the schism cannot really be established. There were conflicts as early as the fourth century, and the break in 1054 was itself followed by centuries of union attempts. Thus a gradual estrangement began very early, and culminated in the high Middle Ages. But the real extent of the tragedy is not taken with enough seriousness even today. Most contemporary historians and theologians view Christianity exclusively in the light of its history in the West, and overlook the importance of the split between Rome and Byzantium. For them, Eastern Christianity is a forever marginalized antique, not substantially different from Roman Catholicism, except for its provincialism, its dependence upon emperors, tsars and dictators and its rabid ritualism.

And yet—recognizing the many ambiguities in the successive historical episodes—East and West were debating the issue which is at the root of all earlier and later Christian divisions: what comes first, the institution guaranteeing the truth, or Truth itself? A common mind on this issue could not be found, and the issue itself was often lost in the pettiness of the debates.

In 1963, however, when these studies were written, the great ecumenical events generated by the Second Vatican Council, called together by Pope John XXIII and continued by Paul VI, seemed to have finally recognized the problem and taken steps towards a solution.

The Roman Catholic Church began to reemphasize conciliarity, to reaffirm the ecclesial context of the Roman primacy, and to redefine itself in a way which took into consideration the views of others, particularly the Orthodox. This does not mean that all the problems were solved by the decrees of Vatican II. Indeed, the texts repeated the affirmation that "the college of the body of bishops has no authority unless it is understood together with the Roman Pontiff...The pope's power of primacy over all, both pastors and faithful, remains whole and intact" (*Lumen Gentium* III, 22). But much was also said about the meaning of the local church, its eucharistic structure, the responsibility of the people of God. It was acknowledged that the *normal* exercise of papal power is to take place not in isolation, but together with the bishops. Furthermore, in meeting the Orthodox ecumenical patriarchs, Pope Paul VI accepted a protocol which emphasized equality and primacy of honor. The texts spoke of "sister-churches," which was symbolically more important than the "lifting of the anathemas" of 1054. The latter gesture only took care of an episode which was not, in any case, the schism itself. It did not resolve other issues, such as the much more significant fact of the anathemas of 1439, levelled against those—i.e., the Orthodox—who did not accept the decrees of the Council of Florence in that year...

As this modest, but still quite important, ecumenical progress was being made, the authors of the book on *The Primacy of Peter* returned to the *sources* of the conflict: the different reading of the scriptural texts, the "eucharistic" ecclesiology of the early Church (which admitted, and even presupposed, the *priority* of some churches, but excluded the *power* of some over the others), and the use made of both scripture and ecclesiology by the Byzantine Orthodox polemicists of the past. Also, the late Nicholas Afanasieff made a serious effort to find a way, within the framework of his eucharistic ecclesiology, to acknowledge a church "presiding in love," and Alexander Schmemann courageously handled the internal problems of contemporary Orthodoxy, determined in part by fear of anything smacking of "papacy," and in fact resulting in a weakening of "universal consciousness," in nationalism and divisiveness.

Is the witness of Orthodox authors, published in 1963, still relevant today? The fact that St Vladimir's Seminary Press has received a growing number of requests for a new edition clearly indicates that it is. I see three main reasons why the questions debated in this book remain of central importance:

1) The Second Vatican Council has raised ecumenical expectations to the point that Christian unity appeared imminent to many. Many within Roman Catholic and Protestant circles, anticipating forthcoming ecclesiastical moves, adopted the practice of intercommunion as a matter of course. Serious theologians suggested immediate practical steps (not realizing how utopian they actually were), such as the recognition of Protestant sacraments and orders by Rome and the participation of Protestants in papal elections.[1] Although the Orthodox generally remained more reserved, the diplomatic ecumenism practiced by the ecumenical patriarchate, as well as some gestures on the part of the Russian church, also created, with the help of the media, an atmosphere of somewhat misleading expectations.

2) Beyond such superficial appearances, an honest and constructive theological dialogue continued throughout the past three decades. Honesty—a really important dimension!—was shown by Pope Paul VI himself, when he said in 1967 that "the pope—as we all know—is undoubtedly the gravest obstacle in the path of ecumenism." What he obviously referred to was the papacy as it exists today, not the Roman primacy of the early centuries. Some Roman Catholic scholars were understanding of the Orthodox objections and looked seriously and responsibly for ways to overcome the gap between two ecclesiologies. André de Halleux examined the real implications of the notion of "sister-churches" as a model for possible reconciliation,[2] and J. M. R. Tillard, while trying to maintain the notion of a Roman primacy which should be more than an "honor," frankly recognized that the "reformed" and truly imperial papacy created by Gregory VII and Boniface VIII "continued to mark the Western Catholic view of the papacy down to our own times," and asked the question: did not the bishop of Rome become "more than a pope," acting "in solitude"?[3] Recent developments

1 Cf. Joseph A. Burgess, "Lutherans and the Papacy," in Peter J. McCord, ed., *A Pope for All Christians? An Inquiry into the Role of Peter in the Modern Church* (New York: Paulist Press, 1975), p. 43.
2 André de Halleux, *Patrologie et oecuménisme. Recueil d'études* (University Press: Leuven, 1990), pp. 518, 555, etc.
3 J. M. R. Tillard, O.P., *The Bishop of Rome*, tr. by John de Satgé (Wilmington, DE: Michael

in Eastern Europe and the support given to "Uniatism" by Rome are obviously seen by most Orthodox as confirming that the medieval "imperial" papacy remains alive even today...

3) There has been no real improvement in the internal problems of the Orthodox world.[4] It is obvious, therefore, that Orthodox theologians should not limit their study of scriptures and the early church to a negative critique of Roman ecclesiology. The unity of each local church, the unity in faith and discipline between local churches, both on the regional and universal level, are what they teach as expressions of true ecclesial communion. All forms of primacy are justifiable only as instruments to secure such communion. What permanent principles and positive models shall the contemporary Orthodox church follow, and are they to be found in the person of the apostle Peter? How is one to approach the problem of apostolic succession?

A wise Italian Roman Catholic layman has recently made a relevant call to avoid "ecumenical triumphalism," "which wavers between steps so little [as] to resemble immobility and such great and definite targets [as] to change themselves into an utopia."[5] Rome and Orthodoxy, whether or not they practice triumphalistic unionism, unavoidably define their ecclesiological positions—and even their internal problems—within the framework of the same scriptures and the same history of the first Christian millennium. This is the true meaning of the assertion that they are indeed "sister-churches." But, between quarrelling "sisters," reconciliation involves many intimate feelings and long-established perceptions. Union can be realized only through ultimate and reciprocal honesty, and readiness to engage in constructive self-criticism.

The present collection of studies might be useful in achieving these goals.

John Meyendorff

Glazier, 1982), pp. 50-60, 193.
4   Cf. J. Meyendorff, "Ecclesiastical Regionalism: Structures of Communion or Cover for Separatism?," in *The Byzantine Legacy in the Orthodox Church* (Crestwood, NY: St Vladimir's Seminary Press, 1982), pp. 217-234.
5   Giuseppe Alberigo, ed., *Christian Unity. The Council of Ferrara-Florence, 1438/9-1989* (Leuven: University Press, 1991), p. 19. This collection of papers, given on the occasion of the 550th anniversary of the Council of Florence, is a mine of information about the failed unionist council.

1

Peter's Place In The Primitive Church

Nicholas Koulomzine

The subject of this article is Peter's position in the early Church, according to the data which the New Testament texts provide.

Peter's history may be divided into three successive stages:

1) Peter in the primitive Church of Jerusalem (Acts 1–5);
2) Peter at the beginning of the spreading of the Gospel (Acts 6–12);
3) Peter after he left Jerusalem.

Our study of Peter's history will thus be limited to the time after Christ's ascension; it will not attempt to study his life while his Divine Master was on earth, nor to give an exegesis of the Gospel texts on which his primacy has been founded.

I

The Church was formed on the day of Pentecost, at Jerusalem. There the Twelve who were the core of this Church found that they must make up their minds about the function to which Christ had called and trained them. The Church of Jerusalem was, for them, the fulfillment of the Messianic Age they had been waiting for. The Book of Acts (our only source for the period) displays Peter as the *Protos*, or First among the Twelve in the heart of their Church. Peter had already taken the initiative of electing the Twelfth Apostle in place of Judas (Acts 1:15–26): he was the one of the Twelve who made the great speech of Pentecost (Acts 2:14–36). He again, in company with John, spoke to the multitude in the temple after the lame man was healed (Acts 3:12–26), and spoke on the next day before the Sanhedrin (Acts 4:8–12). What a striking change from the Simon in the Gospel, the *man of little faith* (Mt 14:31), who had begun to sink in the waters, and still needed his divine Master's prayers to remain steadfast in faith at the last (Lk 22:32)! He had pledged his faith to Jesus and denied Him thrice, and it had been hard for him to believe in the Resurrection.

In the Pentecost speech, after the Holy Spirit had come down, Peter spoke in the name of the Church, and in the name of all the churches still to be established: he made, at that historic moment, the first public confession of the work of Christ, as foretold by the Scriptures; and he proclaimed His Passion, Resurrection, and Ascension into glory. "This Jesus, delivered up according to the definite plan and foreknowledge of God, you crucified and killed by the hands of lawless men. But God raised him up" (Acts 2:23–4). Christ whom the Scriptures promised, "This Jesus God raised up, and of that we are witnesses. Being therefore exalted at the right hand of God, and having received from the Father the promise of the Holy Spirit..." (Acts 2:32–3). For the first time in history, the Twelve, by the mouth of Peter, confess the mystery of the Lord's being glorified, after His Passion and Resurrection: it is the first act of faith under the New Covenant. "Let all the house of Israel therefore know assuredly that God has made him both Lord and Christ, this Jesus whom you crucified" (Acts 2:36).

Long before, at Caesarea Philippi, the Twelve had not understood the mystery of their Master's sufferings and glory; and on the road to Gethsemane they had still, perhaps, not fully understood the scope of the promise assuring to them the Paraclete who would "teach them all things" (Jn 14:26). But now Peter, in the midst of the Twelve, at the Pentecost speech addressing the people gathered in the temple court, proclaims the coming down of the Spirit. He alludes to Joel's prophecy:

And it shall come to pass afterward, that I will pour out my spirit on all flesh; your sons and your daughters shall prophesy, your old men shall dream dreams, and your young men shall see visions. Even upon the menservants and maidservants in those days, I will pour out my spirit. (Joel 2:28–9; Acts 2:17–18)

Peter, like a prophet of old, and being himself a prophet among the other prophets of the New Church, makes the solemn affirmation that Christ, "being therefore exalted at the right hand of God, and having received from the Father the promise of the Holy Spirit...has poured out this which you see and hear" (Acts 2:33). Peter the prophet unveils the hidden meaning of the Scriptures, and reveals in them a plan conceived in the mysterious being of the Trinity. Once the Son has finished His work, the Father exalts Him, and so makes possible the descent of the Holy Spirit. By the mouth of Peter, first among the Twelve, the Church of the New Covenant comes to its first knowledge of the mystery of the Trinity, now fully revealed; so that it may become (as Peter himself will say in his epistle) the Church of the Elect, "chosen and destined by God the Father and sanctified by the Spirit for obedience to Jesus Christ and for sprinkling with his blood" (1 Pet 1:2).

Immediately after the speech, Peter and the Twelve invite those present to be baptized: "Repent and be baptized, every one of you in the name of Jesus Christ...and you shall receive the gift of the Holy Spirit" (Acts 2:38).

Was Peter the first to take the Lord's place at the celebration of the Holy Banquet? New Testament texts do not say so, but the Church's life has always centered on the Eucharist. Peter, in the midst of the Twelve and the first community at Jerusalem, was probably first in breaking the Bread.[1]

Peter is also the first thaumaturge; with John as companion, he performs the cure of the lame man (Acts 3:1ff). He is specially cited among the other miracle-working apostles (Acts 5:12), and even his shadow brings miracles to pass (Acts 5:15). He is also Judge (with the Twelve) in the first community at Jerusalem (the incident of Ananias and Sapphira, Acts 5). It is he who presides, with the Twelve, over the organization and administration of their communal possessions (a charge afterwards entrusted to the Seven by the Twelve, [Acts 2:42; 4:34; see also 6:1]). Finally, Peter is held responsible to answer before the Sanhedrin (accompanied by John in Acts 4 and the other apostles in Acts 5). During the first period in the life of the Mother-Church of Jerusalem, Peter is obviously in the forefront.

But how can we describe his role? The word "head" or "chief" implies a personal power to command, but nothing of the sort is specifically set down by the texts. The word "president" sounds wrong, somehow anachronistic. The title of First Bishop must also be rejected, for this is an absolute anachronism in the early period and takes no account of the role played by the other apostles, among whom Peter is, as it were, *primus*

1   Cf. Nicholas Afanassieff, *The Lord's Table* (Paris, 1952) (in Russian).

inter pares; neither does it recognize what an entirely special and unique situation there was in the Pentecostal Church. Matthew uses no such titles (and his materials and their composition are generally traced to Jerusalem circles): he cites Peter in the list of the Twelve Apostles (Mt 10:2) with the description, or should we say title, of "First"—as though, apparently, it was impossible to describe his position in any better way.

But we must make clear, yet again, that Peter is first of the Twelve, first among the Twelve. The text of Acts confirms this: Peter never acts or speaks alone, but in company with the Twelve, or sometimes John. Luke, presumed author of the Book of Acts, makes this very clear, perhaps by design, in all the texts concerning Peter in the first five chapters.

But there is a further point of definition which we feel is necessary. Peter had to play his role of First among the Twelve within the Pentecostal Church, and at Jerusalem. This role of Peter's was absolutely unique in history, as the Pentecostal Church was also unique in history. The Church would never again be made up so largely of eyewitnesses to the Incarnation and Glorification of the Son; of witnesses to the coming of the Holy Spirit on Pentecost; of witnesses to the Father's revelation in the Son and by the Spirit; of first testifiers to the Trinity. Jerusalem was also unique in having so many gifts of the Holy Spirit, given to so many. It was the pattern for future churches, and a foretaste of the heavenly Jerusalem.

It was in this Pentecostal and unrepeatable Church that Peter stood first among the Twelve. We think that his primacy may properly be discussed only if we regard it in that setting: i.e., in a given church, at a given (and unique) time.

The remaining part of our inquiry is to ask a threefold question: As the Church's history unfolded, what role belonged to Jerusalem, to the Twelve, and to Peter?

II

The first believers expected the Lord's coming from day to day: but history was bound to follow its course. We know the grand outlines of this chiefly by reading the Acts of the Apostles. Luke's method—he is generally considered to be sound historian (cf. Lk 1:1–4)—was to collate and arrange all the information available to him: documents, oral tradition and personal reminiscences. But he still could not avoid making a selection: he recorded the events that illustrated the purpose (or purposes) of his book, stressing this or that matter as important to him. Luke's main purpose in writing Acts was to show Theophilus—probably an influential Greek—how the Good News came to the Gentile world; how the Church of Jerusalem, at first a single body of Jews who respected the law of Moses, afterwards became the Universal Church as he knew it after A.D. 70, when his book was probably composed. Luke's purpose dictated the form of the book, which is:

1) Chs. 1–5: The Church of Jerusalem.

2) Chs. 6–12: The Good News begins to be spread in the world of the Diaspora.

3) Chs. 13–28: Christianity spreads to the Gentile world.

These may conveniently be called the first, second and third periods of first-century history according to Luke's arrangement of Acts: we will add a fourth, beginning after A.D. 70. In the first part of Acts, as we have said above, Luke tells us about the Church of Jerusalem, the Twelve, and Peter. The most important event in this period is Pentecost. In the third period, when the Good News is propagated in the Gentile world, Luke's interest turns to Paul, the apostle to the Gentiles and the great protagonist of the wider evangelism. His arrival in Rome is the logical point to end the book: the Good News, represented by Paul in person, reaches the capital of the empire. The second period must be regarded as a time of transition, a beginning of the spread of the Gospel, but mostly among the Jewish diaspora.

Luke is a historian first, but a theologian as well. The history he writes is the history of the Church, its life and its growth. And he sees, beyond history, the Church's unity in the abiding and life-giving activity of the Holy Spirit.

Can we really say that the Church had a hierarchical structure in the first century? In the second century, St Ignatius of Antioch bears witness in his letters to the existence of local churches, each centered on one particular bishop, accompanied by presbyters, and aided by deacons. But this state of affairs is the final product of a formative period: the list of hierarchical orders had become progressively more uniform. If we speak of hierarchical structure in the Church when its history began, we are in danger of falling into anachronism and of being forced to use inadequate terms. Yet, with all these reservations, we still think we can find, in Acts, pieces of valuable information about the role played by Jerusalem, the Twelve, and Peter. Luke does, of course, schematize and harmonize, unlike Paul, whose epistles are direct evidence. Luke writes later, at a time when the burning questions between Jewish-born and Gentile-born Christians are settled. Some Gnostic doctrines are beginning to creep into the fold, and the Church must now ensure unity and set its house in order. Concern to show that the Church's development was continuous was never out of Luke's mind when he wrote Acts.

One concern is conspicuously absent in his work: he does not try to give us a complete life-picture of any personage, even of Peter or Paul. We should like to be told more about Peter's fate after he left Jerusalem (Acts 12:17), and Paul's after he came to Rome. But Luke was only interested in the roles Peter and Paul played in the Church's history: that Church which, in spite of the world's indifference or enmity, even despite the weaknesses and hesitations of the Christians themselves, ascends the royal road marked out by the feet of Christ and by the direction of the Spirit.

Luke's task as a church historian for the middle period (covered in Acts 6–12), which we are now approaching, was more complicated than it was for the first period. The main subject of these chapters is the spreading of the Gospel in the Jewish world of the Diaspora. This preceded, and made possible, a further transmission of the Good News to the Gentiles.

According to Luke, the spreading of the Gospel outside the bounds of Jerusalem had its starting point in the persecution which followed Stephen's martyrdom. We may take it that this persecution was provoked by the attitude taken by the "Hellenist" members of the Church of Jerusalem[2] (Acts 7:41–53). "And on that day a great persecution arose

---

2   The Hellenists are Jews of the Diaspora, Jewish by religion but Greek-speaking, giving their
     obedience to the hierarchic religious center of Jerusalem. They often had Greek names as well
     as Jewish ones (e.g., John-Mark, Saul-Paul). The early Church of Jerusalem consisted of
     Jewish and Jewish-hellenist converts. Cornelius (ch. 10) was the first Gentile to be converted.

against the church in Jerusalem; and they were all scattered throughout the region of Judaea and Samaria, except the apostles" (Acts 8:1). These "scattered" Christians were, according to Luke, the first to preach the Gospel outside the walls of Jerusalem. Philip was one of them and went to Samaria (ch. 8), where his teaching was crowned with success; and he baptized the Ethiopian. Was Ananias also one of them, the Ananias who received Paul at Damascus? We cannot tell. Were the churches visited by Peter (Acts 9:32–43) evangelized by Christians scattered from Jerusalem? Probably they were. Of one thing we can be sure, "Now those who were scattered because of the persecution that arose over Stephen traveled as far as Phoenicia and Cyprus and Antioch" (Acts 11:19), first preaching only to Jews, but at Antioch to Gentiles also (Acts 11:19–20).

Jerusalem, where the Twelve remained, does not seem at this time to be taking the initiative in evangelization. Their role is described by Luke:

> Now when the apostles at Jerusalem heard that Samaria had received the word of God, they sent to them Peter and John, who came down and prayed for them that they might receive the Holy Spirit; for it had not yet fallen on any of them, but they had only been baptized in the name of the Lord Jesus. Then they laid their hands on them and they received the Holy Spirit. *(Acts 8:14–17)*

The evangelization carried out by others (not the Twelve) does receive something from the center in Jerusalem, namely, confirmation by the laying-on of apostles' hands; thus the new communities, in receiving the Holy Spirit, in turn acquire fullness in their life as churches. "So the church...was built up; and walking in the fear of the Lord and in the comfort of the Holy Spirit it was multiplied" (Acts 9:31). The Twelve were not members of these churches; but acting in the name of Jerusalem, they gave the Holy Spirit to them, and the new churches were born into the graces of the Spirit, as the Mother-Church of Jerusalem was born on the day of Pentecost.

Peter is always in the forefront among the Twelve. He goes to Samaria, his name being paired with John's. Still more significant is his visit to a whole series of churches (see Acts 9:32–43). This is the period when he receives a special revelation from Christ concerning the baptism of Cornelius, the first Gentile to come into the Church. Luke stresses this, and gives a long and detailed account (Acts 10:1–11:18).

It should be noted, however, that Peter's role during this period cannot be dissociated from the role played by the Twelve, and by Jerusalem, any more than it could be in the preceding period, which we have already discussed. In fact it was the Twelve, still in Jerusalem, who dispatched Peter and John to Samaria (Acts 8:14). Again, Jerusalem was the place and the Twelve were the body to which Peter reported on his activities during this period. Luke is careful to point this out: "Now the apostles and the brethren who were in Judaea heard that the Gentiles also had received the word of God. So when Peter went up to Jerusalem, the circumcision party criticized him" (Acts 11:1–2) and reproached him for having eaten with Gentiles. But Peter told of the miracles that had come with Cornelius' conversion, and appeased the assembly (Acts 11:1–18). Peter's dependence on the Twelve and on the Church of Jerusalem is thus very clearly outlined by the author of Acts. When the Gospel began to be propagated outside the bounds of Judaea, Jerusalem still kept its central place among the newly-developing churches. It presided at their birth by sending apostles as representatives. The Twelve still had their seats at Jerusalem and, among them, Peter continued to occupy the first place.

But during this same period a new personage arrives on the historical scene, Saul, the future apostle to the Gentiles. He is first mentioned in the account of Stephen's martyrdom; then he has a vision of Christ while Peter is going round visiting the churches. Subsequently, Paul never loses the conviction that he has received his election from Christ himself, and not from men. He begins his epistle to the Galatians by saying, "Paul an apostle—not from men nor through man, but through Jesus Christ and God the Father, who raised him from the dead" (Gal 1:1). He returns to the point: "For I would have you know, brethren, that the gospel which was preached by me is not man's gospel, nor was I taught it, but it came through a revelation of Jesus Christ" (Gal 1:11–12).[3] Christ's revelation dispensed him from receiving his apostolic power from the hands of the Twelve of Jerusalem. In the same epistle, we read:

> But when he who had set me apart before I was born, and had called me through his grace, was pleased to reveal his son to me, in order that I might preach him among the Gentiles, I did not confer with flesh and blood, nor did I go up to Jerusalem to those who were apostles before me, but I went away into Arabia; and again I returned to Damascus. (Gal 1:15–17)

3   See also 1 Cor 9:1; 5:5-8, and the three accounts of Paul's conversion in Acts 9, 22 and 26.

Christ Himself makes Paul His Apostle.

But Luke, in his concern to show the Church in proper unity and continuity, takes careful note of the fact that Paul did not remain a stranger to the community of Jerusalem. The chronological order of his actions after being baptized is difficult for us to grasp entirely, because it is difficult to coordinate Luke's data with those of Paul himself. Luke tells us that Paul, once converted, turns his eyes towards the center, Jerusalem, where he is presented by Barnabas to the Twelve (Acts 9:26ff). But Paul says in clear terms that he only appeared at Jerusalem three years later, and then paid a visit to Peter alone, and stayed no longer than fifteen days (Gal 1:18). This visit by Paul to Jerusalem was certainly not an act of submission on his part, but much more like an act of communion with the mother-church.

The birth of the Church of Antioch, which was founded by fugitives from the persecution at Jerusalem, is another important event at the end of this period. It was there that the Good News was proclaimed to the Gentiles for the first time, after Cornelius was converted (Acts 11:19–21). Antioch was called to be the center from which Paul would set out to conquer the Gentile world.

Jerusalem was perturbed again, as it had been perturbed when Peter returned after the conversion of Cornelius (Acts 11:1). The man who was sent to the new church this time was not one of the twelve, but a member of their congregation, Barnabas, "a good man, full of the Holy Spirit and of faith" (Acts 11:24). "When he came and saw the grace of God, he was glad; and he exhorted them all to remain faithful to the Lord with steadfast purpose" (Acts 11:23). Barnabas was content to observe the facts and encourage the faithful. One of his first concerns was to find Paul, who had just then retired to Tarsus. Although Jerusalem had been perturbed about what was going on at Antioch, one does have the impression that the Church of Antioch was beginning to feel more independent in its relations with Jerusalem. A personal confirmation by one of the Twelve was no longer seen as mandatory. A new persecution, that of Herod Agrippa (Acts 12:1), marks the end of this period. One of the Twelve, James, the brother of John and son of Zebedee, is the first victim.[4] From this time on, the New Testament

4 Not to be confused with James son of Alpheus, one of the Twelve, nor with James the brother of the Lord, of whom we will presently have more to say.

makes no further mention of a permanent college of the Twelve. After the martyrdom of James, the son of Zebedee, they did not elect a Twelfth, as they had done after the treachery and death of Judas. From now on, throughout the New Testament, the Twelve (or Eleven) are mentioned only twice: first in 1 Cor 15:5, in connection with the appearances of the risen Christ; and a second time in the Apocalypse, which refers to Jerusalem to come (Rev 21:14).

During this persecution, Peter himself was imprisoned; after his miraculous deliverance, he visited the house of Mary, mother of John Mark, and then withdrew from Jerusalem. Acts tells us that Peter departed and went "to another place"—εἰς ἕτερον τόπον (Acts 12:17). "Other," we take it, means "other than Jerusalem."

To conclude our examination of this second period in the Church's life, we feel that we may fairly state the following: Jerusalem still presided at the birth of the first local churches outside the territory of Judaea; it remained to a degree the hierarchic center for these churches, so long as the Twelve continued in their seats. Peter always held first place among the Twelve, but the role he played in the Church was still bound up with that of the Twelve and Jerusalem. We have observed, though, that the birth of the Church of Antioch and the coming of Paul already signify that a new period is about to begin.

III

We come now to the third historical period, which begins with Herod's persecution, and to its chief results, the death of James, the son of Zebedee, and Peter's departure; it ends with the destruction of Jerusalem.

Luke, in the Book of Acts, is still our principal source of information (chs. 13–28). His interest is focused almost exclusively on Paul, and he ends his story when Paul reaches Rome, an event that marked (or so he thought) the unmistakable establishment of Christianity in the Gentile world.

The epistles that were written during this third period fill in and clarify the historical picture given by Luke. (Paul is the chief author, but Peter, Jude and James contribute in a smaller way.)

We have been trying to show that Peter's primacy is supported by

New Testament witness during the period when he was in the midst of the Twelve at Jerusalem, and within the Pentecostal Church: there is still support for it during the second, or intermediate period, insofar as the Twelve still retain their seats at Jerusalem. Now we must try to see whether this state of affairs continued during the third period; and we must study the New Testament data on three subjects in turn—Peter, the Twelve, and the Church of Jerusalem.

i. The Itinerant Ministry of Peter and Paul

Paul's activities are better known to us and may be briefly outlined as follows. He makes three missionary journeys, as Luke relates in Acts. After the first, there is the Antioch incident which sets Paul against Peter (Acts 15:1–3 and Gal 2:11–14); there is also the Council of Jerusalem (Acts 15:4–35 and Gal 2:1–10). After his third journey, Paul is arrested at Jerusalem; then, for nearly two years, he remains at Caesarea in chains (Acts 21:17–24). When Festus takes the place of Felix and becomes Procurator of Judaea, Paul appeals to Caesar for judgment and is transferred to Rome (Acts 25).

We will assume that Paul wrote the two epistles to the Thessalonians during his second journey, and that his four great epistles[5] were dispatched in the course of his third journey: after his transfer to Rome and during his two years' captivity (Acts 28:30–1), he wrote the four "captivity epistles."[6] Considering the historical data and the new geographical allusions we find in Paul's so-called "pastoral" epistles,[7] we may allow ourselves to suppose that Paul made at least one other missionary journey. He was to die a martyr at Rome after a second arrest. If it is ever possible to say that the Epistle to the Hebrews was written under the personal inspiration of Paul, then its composition must be dated to the very end of the Apostle's life.[8]

We have much less information about Peter's fate after he left Jerusalem (Acts 12:17). Local tradition in the Church of Rome strongly asserts

---

5 In order of their appearance in the New Testament, the epistles to the Romans, 1 Corinthians, 2 Corinthians, and Galatians.

6 Again in order of New Testament placement, Ephesians, Philippians, Colossians, and Philemon.

7 1 Timothy, 2 Timothy, and Titus.

8 For details, see Bishop Cassian, *Khristos i pervoe khristianskoe pokolenie* (Paris, 1950).

that Peter died a martyr at Rome. But the New Testament gives us only one indication of his presence in the capital city, and that is the mention of Babylon as the place from which the first Epistle was sent out. "She [the Church] who is at Babylon, who is likewise chosen, sends you greetings" (1 Pet 5:13). This precious bit of information supports the tradition, but it only concerns the end of Peter's life; the epistle was probably sent out in the late sixties, possibly after the death of Paul.[9]

Where did Peter go after he left Jerusalem? (Acts 12:17). The New Testament text does not tell us. It does not say that Peter appeared at Rome immediately. On the contrary, we next find him at Antioch, at the time of the controversy when he and Paul were set against each other; and Paul is the one who reports the fact in Gal 2:11–14.

We again find Peter at Jerusalem for the Council, where he defends Paul and Barnabas, who are in trouble with their Jerusalem brethren, so zealous for the law of Moses. We shall have more to say about this council later on.

We are told that Peter had disciples within the Church of Corinth (1 Cor 1:12; 3:22), but this cannot be taken to prove that Peter ever made a personal visit to Corinth.

Peter was not at Rome during Paul's third journey; for the Epistle to the Romans, so rich in greetings to Paul's many friends in the capital, does not mention Peter's name at all. There is a further valuable detail to add from the same epistle: Paul apologizes for not having visited the Romans; he wanted to, but he felt scruples against building "upon another man's foundation" (Rom 15:20). Had Peter been the "other man," Paul's pen would have written the Great Apostle's name almost unbidden; for it would have strengthened his argument.

When Paul later on came to Rome in chains, Luke does not mention Peter's name in the list of "brethren" who went to meet him. And the omission is significant, for it is supported by the silence of the captivity epistles, written by Paul from Rome in the course of the next two years.

In the period before Paul's death, Peter's name is again not mentioned, not only in the pastoral epistles, but also—and this means more—in the Epistle to the Hebrews, written at Rome in the name of

9 Cassian, *ibid.*, p. 291.

"those who come from Italy" (Heb 13:24).

After that, there is only the evidence of 1 Peter 5:1, which concerns Peter's life later on, when Paul had perhaps departed to another world.

The general rules say that arguments from silence are not sufficient to provide a positive datum. But in Peter's case, the omissions we spoke of may be of some value. One conclusion seems to be obvious. Peter's work, after he left Jerusalem (Acts 12:17), was no longer tied to a single place on the map, or to a special church.

Jerusalem, in any case, cannot have been the permanent seat of Peter, since James, the brother of the Lord, is always the one called leader of the church once Peter has departed. As for Antioch, the church there was certainly not of Peter's foundation (Acts 11:19–30). Neither was he one of the group that appointed Paul and Barnabas to go on their first mission (Acts 13:1–3). Peter must have really been at Antioch, or Paul would not have emphatically said so (cf. the controversy with Peter, Gal 2:11–14); but Acts never refers to Peter's being at Antioch, so it must have been a passing visit.

There are two possible hypotheses for Peter's presence at Rome: either he went there often, and was often away, or else he arrived very late (perhaps after the death of Paul). In either case, it is an impossibility that Peter had a permanent seat at Rome.

Everything leads us to think that Peter's ministry was peripatetic. His work did not install him as head of any given local church. Did he join the *collegium* of elders in the various churches that he was led to visit? When he came to Rome, he called himself "fellow elder" (1 Pet 5:1). These are words of shining humility when the great Apostle speaks them; but surely they prove just the opposite—that his real title as Christ's Apostle placed him in a much higher position than that of a mere elder in a local church.

We believe that this is a reasonable way to speak of the Apostle Peter; but in Paul's case it is self-evident. We need not bother to give examples to show that the Apostle to the Gentiles claimed no part in the local hierarchies of any of the churches which he founded. As an Apostle of Christ, his ministry was by nature an itinerant ministry and set him above the several churches. He laid his hands upon the elders of these churches, sent letters to some of them, gave them counsel and, indeed, commands, and reserved to himself the right to excommunicate. Peter had acted in this way during the second period, of which we know more and have already spoken. He paid visits to the churches that he did not belong to and, like Paul, he had the right to excommunicate (Simon Magus in Samaria, Acts 8). Surely his apostolic activity after Acts 12:17 continued along the same lines.

ii. The Apostles. The Twelve

Peter, one of the Twelve and first of the Twelve at Jerusalem, afterwards had to fulfill his mission as an Apostle of Christ. So the two terms, "Apostle" and "Twelve," deserve our special consideration.

All four evangelists very frequently use the word μαθητής for the disciples of Christ: and δώδεκα for that inner circle, the Twelve. But the word ἀπόστολος is very rarely used. John's Gospel uses it only once, and to mean envoy, not Apostle; the noun is common, but not the title properly given to the Twelve. "A servant is not greater than his master; nor is he who is sent (ἀπόστολος) greater than he who sent him" (Jn 13:16). In Mark, too, the word appears only once, when the Twelve come back from the mission on which Christ had sent them: "The apostles returned to Jesus" (Mk 6:30)—but it can equally well be translated "and they that were sent...," meaning those whom Christ had sent on a mission. In the Gospel according to Matthew, *apostle* occurs once alone and clearly designates the Twelve by their title: "The names of the twelve apostles are these" (Mt 10:2). So in each of these three Gospels, there is no more than one (or at most two) texts where *apostle* is used to name the Twelve by their proper title. We should also notice at once how often the verb ἀποστέλλω recurs in the Gospels, and how much evidence there is of the *disciples* being sent on missions.

Luke's Gospel, on the other hand, uses ἀπόστολος a number of times, five of which apply clearly and unequivocally to the Twelve (Lk 6:13; 9:10; 17:5; 22:14; 24:10); and one time it is used in a more general sense (Lk 11:49).

The word hardly appears in the first two Gospels, which were composed before A.D. 70, and whose source-material was drawn, directly or indirectly, from the stock teaching for catechumens at Jerusalem. This permits us to suppose that in the early history of the Church the word *Apostle* was not commonly used to describe the Twelve.

In Luke's Gospel, however (generally thought to have been written after A.D. 70), the word is there, a proof, surely, that it became the proper title for the Twelve at some particular time—probably in the third period. The Book of Acts gives confirmation to this hypothesis: Luke uses the word *Apostle* almost exclusively to describe the Twelve. And it is Luke alone who considers it necessary to explain in his Gospel that the title *Apostle* was bestowed on the Twelve by Christ in person. After giving a list of the Twelve, Luke goes on to say "twelve, whom he named apostles" (6:13). Matthew and Mark forgot to put this in, but this is easy to explain: the substance of both Gospels was based on the instruction given to catechumens at Jerusalem in those early days when they still spoke of the disciples, the twelve disciples, and the Twelve. The additional detail provided by Luke points to a time when the Twelve are already commonly named Apostles, and when they find themselves ready to enact the part for which Christ had trained them.

The Pauline writings provide us with additional information, all of which seems to strengthen our theory. Of course the great Apostle to the Gentiles had a striking personality, which put him in a different position from the group of the Twelve Apostles; but the way he himself uses the word Apostle is indirect evidence of how it was used in the third historical period, which is our present concern. Paul does not regularly call himself Apostle (or rather Apostle of Christ) before his third missionary journey: from then onwards, it comes in the headings of all his Epistles (except Hebrews, which does not carry the author's name or—*a fortiori*—his title, and is certainly not Paul's handiwork). In the text of one of Paul's first two Epistles, which were written as early as the second journey, there is some ground (1 Thess 2:6–7) for thinking that the name "Apostle" was used to designate Paul, Sylvanus and Timothy, since their names are all in the heading. Osty translates: "*Nous aurions pu nous donner de l'importance en notre qualité d'Apôtres du Christ*" ["We could have made our weight felt as Apostles of Christ"].

"Apostle of Christ" is the description Paul systematically gives himself from his third journey on, and as he writes, it gradually begins to emerge as a title that ranks him with the Twelve: but he called them such names as "the superlative Apostles" (2 Cor 11:5; 12:11) or "those who were Apostles before me" (Gal 1:17). In the mass of Pauline texts again, the word *Apostle* is not confined to the Twelve, nor to Paul. We can read him speaking of "apostles of the churches" (2 Cor 8:23). And who, incidentally, were "all the apostles" to whom the risen Christ appeared? (1 Cor 15:7). Does "us apostles" in 1 Cor 4:9 mean Paul and Apollos? The text of Rom 16:7 is not very clear, but the word *Apostle* may describe men other than the Twelve. And Paul, in passages like Eph 2:20; 3:5; 4:11, evidently did not rank the Twelve alone with the prophets and teachers.

We need not work out the meaning of *apostle* in detail: we are content to assume, on the basis of the Pauline writings, that this name was gradually given to a circle wider than the Twelve—this happened during the third period. When the Good News began to spread outside Jerusalem and beyond Judaea, it is probable that Jerusalem first, and other churches later, sent out missionaries—envoys, apostles. And it was probably not until the Twelve began to leave Jerusalem, to become missionaries as well, that their position as apostles or envoys took shape. Then was the time for them to carry out their divine Master's injunction and preach even to the ends of the earth.

"The Twelve" is a term which gradually fades from the New Testament vocabulary, as we can all observe. After Herod's persecution, the death of one of the Twelve, and Peter's departure (Acts 12), the question of keeping up a permanent *collegium* of Twelve never comes up again anywhere in the New Testament. Luke has no new story about a second election of a Twelfth. As we have already said, from this point on the Twelve (or Eleven) are only mentioned twice more in the whole New Testament: first by Paul, when he recounts the appearance of the risen Christ (1 Cor 15:5); and once more in John's Apocalypse (21:14), in a description of the heavenly Jerusalem. The Twelve, as a *collegium*, vanish from the scene of Church history from the third period onwards. The New Testament mentions only Peter's departure (Acts 12:17) and the death of James, son of Zebedee. No texts tell us when the ten others left Jerusalem, what roads they took; nor are we told the story of their apostolic lives (apart from what little information we can glean about John).

The only point we can make with confidence is this: they became

Apostles, and that among other apostles, whom the churches had previously sent on missions.

With regard to the fourth period (after A.D. 70), Luke's writings show a tendency to keep the title of Apostles for the Twelve alone: this is clear in the Gospel, and borne out by Acts, where the word is used frequently and almost always to describe the Twelve. There is one notable exception in chapter 14, where the title is applied to Paul and Barnabas (in verse 4 and perhaps also verse 14). This exception again supports my assertion that the field of those qualified to be Apostles had spread, in the third period, to a circle wider than the Twelve; on the other hand, Luke generally reserves this title for the Twelve, which may be evidence of a similarly restrictive tendency, general in the Church during the fourth period (after A.D. 70). The few uses of ἀπόστολος found in New Testament texts of the fourth period rather confirm this,[10] though we cannot say that every writer had as much a tendency as St Luke to reserve this title for the Twelve.

iii. Jerusalem in the Third Period

After Peter leaves (Acts 12:17), James is the one always mentioned as head of the Church of Jerusalem. Traditional exegesis in the Eastern Church has always agreed that this James was the "brother of the Lord," and not James, son of Alpheus, one of the Twelve. In the West, both persons were confusedly called James the Lesser, as opposed to James the Greater, son of Zebedee, who died a martyr's death under Herod (Acts 12:2). Today some Western exegetes have come over to the view that James, the leader of the congregation at Jerusalem, is indeed the "brother of the Lord," and not James, son of Alpheus, whose fate is as little known to us as that of most of the Twelve.

During our Lord's life on earth, his "brethren" remained skeptical. Afterwards, James is listed by Paul in the number of those to whom the risen Christ appeared (1 Cor 15:7). The brethren of the Lord are mentioned in Luke beside the Twelve, before Pentecost (Acts 1:14). Finally, James is mentioned by Paul after his first visit to Jerusalem (Gal 1:19), as an important member of the congregation, even before Peter's departure.

10 1 Pet 1:1; 2 Pet 1:1; 3:2; Jude 17: Rev 2:2; 18:20; 21:14.

Peter, in announcing his departure, addressed James specifically (Acts 12:17). Henceforward James is always referred to as leader of the Church of Jerusalem, and these references are constant and numerous. One New Testament text seems to call him an Apostle: "But I saw none of the other apostles except James the Lord's brother," says Paul (Gal 1:19). The text can also be translated "but only James the Lord's brother," as Osty has noticed; and the French Jerusalem Bible in fact adopts this translation; this means that he is not in the list of the Apostles. There are two other New Testament texts which also seem to exclude James from the rank of Apostle: 1 Cor 9:5; 15:7. As we said above, the apostolic ministry was peripatetic; but James' position at Jerusalem was naturally bound up with one particular local church. He was given a place above the other presbyters of that church, and he acted as their superior (Acts 21:18). Proof that the presbyters existed in the third period is abundantly given by Paul and by Luke. The word ἐπίσκοπος was also used, during this period, to describe a presbyter, as a careful reading of some texts will show (see Acts 15:17 and 20:28 put together; also Tit 1:5–9). Whether there were bishops, in the later sense of the word, as heads of local churches, is a question for which we have no evidence in the third period. But the role that James played at Jerusalem, after Peter had gone, was surely very comparable to the role bishops were to play later on: a lifelong and continuous place as leader of a local church, with a group of presbyters in support. James may not have been called a bishop, but he was in fact the first monarchical bishop of a local church.

A further question must now be tackled: what was Jerusalem's position *vis-à-vis* the other churches? We have already tried to show that it continued as the hierarchical center throughout the second period, and that the new congregations felt their dependent relationship towards the mother-church. This authority belonged to Jerusalem because the Twelve were there, and the first persecution did not dislodge them—an authority wielded by the Twelve, with Peter still the first among them. But as we have already pointed out, the end of this period saw the birth of the Church of Antioch and Paul's appearance on the scene, both of which were signs that a new period was beginning.

History really takes a new direction in the third period, after Peter's departure. Paul and Barnabas, after staying awhile at Antioch, are sent on a mission, and Jerusalem has no part in sending them. Although Luke begins by mentioning the close ties between Antioch and Jerusalem later, life at Antioch seems to go on by itself, independently of Jerusalem. At the very time when Jerusalem is built up as a local church with James at the helm, the Church of Antioch also begins its own life as an independent local church; but it has no sovereign bishop to govern it at this time, as far as we know; churches founded by Paul generally do not either. Formerly, Peter and John were sent on a mission by the Twelve in Jerusalem; now Paul and Barnabas are also sent on a mission by the Church of Antioch (or rather by various prophets and teachers, possibly from Jerusalem but at this time settled in Antioch). While Paul and Barnabas are still on this first missionary journey, Luke, as we noted above, describes them as apostles—a word which in Luke's vocabulary is confined to the Twelve of Jerusalem, apart from this passage (see Acts 14:4, and perhaps 14, where the text is uncertain). Jerusalem is still, to Christian hearts and memories, the mother-church, the place of Pentecost, and the first to send out missionaries. But after Peter leaves, and James, son of Zebedee, dies, the Twelve cease to exercise their authority from Jerusalem. The community led by James, the brother of the Lord is the earliest, chronologically, of all the local churches to be revered by all, but without any direct authority over the other churches: these, later in the first century, are gradually to follow the new pattern and turn into local churches, each with one sovereign bishop as leader.

The story of the Council of Jerusalem (Acts 15 and Gal 2) is of special interest to us because of the information it gives on Jerusalem's position, and on the part its church played in the third period. Paul and Barnabas, once they were back from their first mission and had preached to the Gentiles, naturally came back to Antioch, whose mission had been laid upon them. And there, at Antioch, a serious controversy took place between Paul and Barnabas on one side, and "certain men who came down from Judaea," members of James' congregation, on the other. The issue was whether it was obligatory, for Gentiles coming into the church, first to submit to the Law of Moses and be circumcised (Acts 14:27–15:2). This is no longer the Church of Jerusalem saying, through the Twelve, that it is perturbed about what Paul and Barnabas had done, as they had been perturbed in the second period by Peter's actions after the conversion of Cornelius (Acts 11:1), or by the preaching to the Greeks at Antioch (Acts 11:19–26). The issue was raised by zealots for the law of Moses, not by the Church of Jerusalem as such. We may even suppose that this controversy was the background to Peter's opposition to Paul at Antioch[11] (Gal 2:11–14). In order to end the discussion and stop the disturbance caused by the judaizing agitators "it was resolved" (we could also translate "*they* resolved") to present their case at Jerusalem before the apostles and presbyters (Acts 15:2). Now the call does not come from Jerusalem: Antioch, the Church of Antioch, decides. The decision was not taken on the basis of Jerusalem's rights, or its authority as a hierarchic center. It was a difficult time, and the Council's decision was needed to decide the Church's future; so they decided to go together to the place where the Holy Spirit came down and founded the church; and so the Council dared to conclude with "it seemed good to the Holy Spirit and to us..."

New troubles arose at Jerusalem, caused by Christians brought up with a background of Pharisaism (Acts 15:5–6): further vociferous charges were brought against Paul and Barnabas. The Apostles and presbyters met together to sift things out (Acts 15:6). Peter took the same side as Paul and Barnabas. When the discussion was at its height—and it seems to have been stormy—he rose to speak. Peter was first to intervene, and with authority, but his action was not based on his present position in the Church. He explained it by referring to his own past: "Brethren, you know that in the early days God made choice among you, that by my mouth the Gentiles should hear the word of the gospel and believe" (Acts 15:7); this probably alludes to the baptism of Cornelius' household, which happened in such special circumstances that Peter had to explain them to the Twelve at Jerusalem.

> And God who knows the heart bore witness to them, giving them the Holy Spirit just as he did to us; and he made no distinction between us and them, but cleansed their hearts by faith. Now therefore why do you make trial of God by putting a yoke upon the neck of the disciples which neither our fathers nor we have been able to bear? But we believe that we shall be saved through the grace of the Lord Jesus, just as they will. (Acts 15:8–11)

11 We are supposing that Gal 2:11–14 should be read not as a sequel to the first part of the epistle, which is historical in character, but as a beginning of Paul's argument. This is not the only possible hypothesis.

"And all the assembly kept silence" (Acts 15:12). Peter's intervention had restored peace. Paul and Barnabas were able to take a turn in speaking "as they related what signs and wonders God had done through them among the Gentiles" (Acts 15:12).

When the assembly again held their peace, it was James' turn to have the last word. He repeats Peter's arguments in justification of Paul and Barnabas and supports them by a quotation from Isaiah, thus bringing the debate to a most solemn conclusion—"official" would be the modern word. "Therefore my judgment is that we should not trouble those of the Gentiles who turn to God" (Acts 15:19). Peter's intervention may seem to have carried more weight in the meeting, but the presidency of the assembly belonged to James alone. Peter had the authority to bear witness to past events, so he took on himself the main role in defense of Paul and Barnabas; but James, in the first person, pronounced the final judgment. This role was his by right of place, for he was inside the local church of Jerusalem and placed at its head (with the presbyters supporting him) ever since Peter had gone (Acts 12:17). Because James was thus placed at Jerusalem, any assembly that met there had to have him as its president, in spite of persons such as Peter having great authority. The fact that James did preside at the Council of Jerusalem and afterwards did not in any way weaken the supremacy of the Apostles over the churches they had already founded. The text of the letter to "the brethren who are of the Gentiles" (Acts 15:23–9) in Antioch, Syria, and Cilicia was not signed by James, whose writ ran in Jerusalem alone; the letter was from the Apostles and presbyters.

There is an echo of this meeting in Paul. Galatians 2:1–10 is generally considered to be a parallel to Acts 15. Paul's style in reporting the events is quite different; but, after all, Luke writes as a church historian, whereas Paul's report is made in the course of a fervent defense against the judaizing agitators in Galatia. Paul makes a point of declaring that he went up to Jerusalem because he had received a revelation: this means, in the context, that he was not ordered to go by "those who were of repute" (Gal 2:2). Paul continues in Gal 2:6–10:

And from those who were reputed to be something (what they were makes no difference to me; God shows no partiality)—those, I say, who were of repute added nothing to me; but on the contrary, when they saw that I had been entrusted with the gospel to the uncircumcised, just as Peter had been entrusted with the gospel to the circumcised (for he who worked through Peter for the mission to the circumcised worked through me also for the Gentiles), and when they perceived the grace that was given to me, gave to me and Barnabas the right hand of fellowship, that we should go to the Gentiles and they to the circumcised; only they would have us remember the poor, which very thing I was eager to do.

The circumstances under which the two accounts were composed were different, and this explains some of the discordances. Their agreement, on more points than one, seems worthy of our interest: in both accounts, Jerusalem takes no initial step in convoking the assembly; the Apostle Paul makes no submission to the authority of Jerusalem; equal rights are confirmed for Paul on his side and the "pillars" on theirs; and James is first to be named in the list of "pillars" when Paul meets them at Jerusalem. The two accounts are strikingly different in character, but they agree about the essential facts for the purposes of the present inquiry.[12]

During his third journey Paul certainly had the poor people of Jerusalem in his heart, and he organized collections for their benefit. Luke mentions this several times, and so does Paul himself. But, here again, this does not mean that Paul is making an act of submission to Jerusalem. On the contrary, the natural thing to think, surely, is that Paul, the Apostle to the gentiles but himself a Jew, has a heartfelt desire to work for the unity of the Christian world.

This analysis of the Church of Jerusalem, and its position during the third period, needs a few words of conclusion. We believe we are now justified in stating that the Church of Jerusalem is no longer a center or seat of authority of the Universal Church. It turns into the first organized local church, under the authority of James, the "brother" of the Lord, who was honored by later Orthodox tradition as first Bishop of Jerusalem.

iv. Conclusion

In studying this third period in the history of the primitive Church, we

12 It needs to be observed that Luke's account of the Council of Jerusalem, in a quite special way, has attracted criticism even from the milder school. Without describing this criticism in detail, let us only remark that it is not an impossible supposition to say: Luke, who tended to harmonize and systematize, may have mixed two distinct events into one account: (1) a Council in the second period to discuss the Gentiles, with Peter presiding, and (2) a decision made by James inside the Church of Jerusalem at a later date, which Paul would not have known about until he visited Jerusalem for the last time. If we accept this possibility, our argument will gain in strength.

have tried to show successively: (i) that Peter's ministry, after he left Jerusalem, was a roving ministry like that of Paul, and that it did not bind Peter to any local churches he may have founded or visited; (ii) that the role of the Twelve as a *collegium* of twelve was limited in time to the first and second periods; (iii) in the third period Jerusalem lost the position of being the hierarchical center, and became a local church among all of the local churches.

At Jerusalem, then, Peter's primacy, which we began by considering, was a primacy within the Twelve, tied to the presence of the Twelve and the birth of the Pentecostal Church. Peter's primacy, thus taken, is tied to a particular role and to fixed historical conditions of a unique kind: this view finds wide support in the New Testament writings, as the beginning of our essay shows.

But as historical conditions changed, and Peter left Jerusalem, he no longer figured as one of the Twelve: he became a roving apostle. The Twelve no longer formed a *collegium* at Jerusalem, so the city lost its position as hierarchical center. Given these new historical conditions, is it still possible to speak of the primacy of Peter? The New Testament texts in no way show that it is.

This short study of Peter's place in the Church does not claim, of course, to have exhausted the subject of Peter's primacy in its entirety. But the Gospel texts, generally used as the basis for such discussion, are made clearer by being read in the light of the Great Apostle's life-history.

For Peter's actions after Ascension give us a means to discover the real meaning of the words that Christ had spoken to him. Jerusalem is the place where Peter stands forth, in the Pentecostal Church and surrounded by the Twelve (he is never dissociated from them in the Gospels); here he first shows that he can be a Rock, the Rock of the Church, as Christ called him when He said, "You are Peter, and on this rock I will build my Church" (Mt 16:18). At Jerusalem, again, Peter is to show a faith that does not fail, and acts out Christ's promise, "And when you have turned again, strengthen your brethren" (Lk 22:32). And, still at Jerusalem, Peter becomes the Shepherd of the Church and carries out Christ's injunction, "Feed my lambs, feed my sheep" (Jn 21:15–17).

The Gospel of the Church of Jerusalem, St Matthew's, is furthermore the

Gospel which underlines Peter's primacy and places him apart in the list of the Twelve (Mt 10:2). It is Matthew who reports the solemn word of Christ, "You are Peter, and on this rock I will build my Church" (Mt 16:18).

2

Peter's Primacy In The New Testament And The Early Tradition

Veselin Kesich

Claims that the Church of Rome has a special status are based upon a specific understanding of the role and position of Peter in relation to Jesus, the twelve apostles, and the early church. The Apostle Peter was the leading disciple of Jesus and the best known figure in the earliest Christian communities. After the death and resurrection of Christ, he was known to Christians as the leader, the shepherd, the missionary in Jerusalem, Antioch and Rome—the three most important centers of primitive Christianity. Other churches in the Hellenistic world, in Corinth and Asia Minor, were also acquainted with the life and work of the apostle. Wherever the story of Jesus' life and ministry was told, Peter was remembered as the witness to the gospel's words and events, and as the head of the first Christian community.

Our purpose in the present article is to examine the question of how the New Testament and the early Christian writers of the second and third centuries understood the role and the place of Peter. In our discussion, we will focus on Mt 16:17–19, for it is the most crucial passage on which claims for Peter's special status have been based. We will also be obliged to relate this text to other references to Peter, for the apostle did not live in isolation. Nothing about Peter can be separated from historical happenings in the crucial decades of the first century.

I

The place and role of the Apostle Peter during the public ministry of Jesus, as well as in the first-century church, have been of vital importance for all Christians. To clarify the main issues regarding Peter's position and function in this formative period, we must turn first to our primary sources—the Gospels and the Book of Acts—to recapture the person of

Peter, as well as the pattern of life and relationship within the Apostolic Church. Only by analyzing the evidence provided in the documents of the first century, which are accepted as canonical by all Christian churches, can we hope to enter into their perspective in our search for an understanding of the problem that confronts us even today.

It is a widely accepted hypothesis among modern scholars that Mark's Gospel is the earliest of our four gospels, and John's the latest, and that the evangelists Matthew and Luke were acquainted with Mark and drew upon it, while John's is based upon traditions independent of the three synoptic gospels. As we attempt to present an image of Peter, we shall accept these assumptions. We must be aware, however, that we are dealing here with working hypotheses of modern scholarship, and not with dogmas. We recognize that there are other theories about the formation of the Gospel tradition, but as far as our question is concerned—the role and place of Peter—both the more traditional scholarly interpretation and those challenging it bring us essentially to the same portrait of the apostle.

Let us begin with the Gospel of Mark. Peter, or Simon, with his brother Andrew, is the first to be called to follow Jesus (Mk 1:16); his name comes at the head of the list of the twelve, "Simon whom he surnamed Peter" (Mk 3:16). He is the spokesman for the group of the disciples (Mk 10:28). He is the first to confess that Jesus is the Christ (Mk 8:27–30). Just as the other members of the twelve, he misunderstands Jesus' mission. When Peter rebukes Jesus for saying that it is necessary for the Son of Man to suffer and to die, Jesus turns and looks at the other disciples (Mk 8:33) before answering Peter: "Get behind me Satan! For you are not on the side of God, but of men." The other disciples share the thinking that Peter expresses. Although Peter is often "the embodiment" of the misunderstanding and failure of Jesus' disciples (Mk 9:2–13; 14:32–42, 14:50), he is nevertheless presented in this gospel as the most prominent in the college of the twelve and as their spokesman.[1] In time of crisis, all the disciples forsake Jesus and flee.

1   Raymond E. Brown, Karl P. Donfried, and John Reumann, eds., *Peter in the New Testament* (Minneapolis, 1973), p. 61. This book is a collaborative assessment, by Roman Catholic and Protestant scholars, of the role of Peter, which presupposes "the attitudes and methods common in contemporary biblical criticism" (p. 7).

    Joseph A. Burgess, *A History of the Exegesis of Matthew 16:17–19 from 1781 to 1965* (Ann Arbor, 1976), gives a valuable history of the interpretation of the central Petrine passage. In

Peter's denial, however, is described in all four gospels in some detail. And yet, after the resurrection on the first day of the week, the angel announces to the women, who are amazed to find the tomb empty, that Jesus of Nazareth is risen and commands them to "Go, tell his disciples and Peter that he is going before you to Galilee" (Mk 16:7). Again, Peter is specifically mentioned here. The Gospel of Mark ends with the women fleeing from the tomb. They are in awe. There is no specific list of Christ's post-resurrection appearances in this gospel. The so-called "longer ending" of Mark (16:9–20) is most probably a later composition, and our important ancient codices, the Codex Vaticanus and the Codex Sinaiticus, do not contain it. If the gospel ends at 16:8, then the verse that precedes it may reflect the evangelist's knowledge of Peter as the first witness to the resurrection.[2]

the preface he notes that by following the history of this passage, we are introduced into "the history of the Christian Church from a restricted but often illuminating perspective." While centering on the clash of ideas and interpretations between Roman Catholics and Protestants, Burgess makes an effort to define the main attitudes of certain Orthodox scholars, while noting their limited involvement in biblical exegesis. As there is no comprehensive study of the Orthodox history of the interpretation of Mt 16:17–19, Roman Catholic scholars have tried to fill the gap, according to Burgess. The practice of collecting material from Orthodox dogmatic and liturgical sources "in order to prove to the Orthodox that originally their teachers and liturgy accepted the primacy of the pope," Burgess notes, goes back to the middle of the seventeenth century. At the time of the First Vatican Council in 1870, this claim intensified. In our own time, the ecumenical movement has affected Roman Catholic research, and Wilhelm de Vries, the authority on the problem of primacy, maintains that "this polemical attitude" of trying to prove that the Orthodox Churches ever accepted the primacy of the Pope is useless. He has met with opposition from other Roman Catholic scholars, who still cling to the old attitude (pp. 21ff).

In his search for spokesmen of modern Orthodoxy and its views on Mt 16:17–19, Burgess pays particular attention to the Russian theologians who were forced to settle in Western Europe after the Revolution of 1917. Burgess sees their traditional attitude toward this text as a reflection of their noninvolvement in modern historical biblical exegesis. Bishop Cassian "is the only one among the Russian Orthodox who has been affected at all by modern historical exegesis" (see pp. 155–157).

2   R. E. Brown, Donfried, Reumann, pp. 70ff. Paul handed on to the Corinthians what he himself had received, that Christ died for our sins, was buried, was raised on the third day, and that "he appeared to Cephas, then to the twelve." After appearing to "more than five hundred brethren...he appeared to James, then to all the Apostles" (1 Cor 15:3–7). E. Stauffer (*Jesus and His Story* [London, 1960] pp. 122, 182) thinks that these verses (5 and 7) suggest the existence of two separate lists of witnesses. First we have Cephas and the twelve, and second, James and all the Apostles. These two competing lists, Stauffer believes, reflect the ancient dispute between Peter and James. But we have no evidence in the New Testament of such a dispute.

According to the longer ending of Mark (16:9), Jesus "appeared first to Mary Magdalene,

The portrait of Peter in this gospel is both "positive" and "negative." It reveals the leading disciple of Jesus as a man who, in spite of his shortcomings, "has left everything" to follow Christ (Mk 10:28), and who became with Andrew a fisher of men (Mk 1:16). E. Stauffer has noted that, unless the Risen Lord had appeared to Peter before all others, unless he had established him again, Peter's role after the denial in the primitive church would have been a riddle. "For Peter was not the kind of man to create this position for himself by the strength of his personality," he concludes.[3]

The evangelist Matthew follows Mark in describing Peter in a position of leadership and prominence. At some points in the first gospel, the priority of Peter is stressed even more than in Mark. Peter's name appears "first" in the list of the twelve apostles (Mt 10:2). Matthew also adds three new passages where Peter is singled out: Mt 14:28–31; 16:17–19; 17:24–27. These passages have no parallels in the other synoptic gospels.[4] In the first passages we see Peter walking on the water but collapsing when confronted with the wind. He became afraid and started to sink. Jesus saved him and said, "O man of little faith, why did you doubt?" (14:31). "Little faith" (ὀλιγόπιστε) is faith that knows fear, hesitant faith. The second Matthean passage (16:17–19) is undoubtedly the most important single text for the primacy of Peter in the New Testament, and due to its significance we shall devote particular attention to it in the next section of this article. And in the third pericope, which refers to the temple tax (17:24–27), preeminence is again given to

from whom he had cast out seven demons" (Jn 20:11–18 agrees with Mk 16:9). Mary Magdalene, however, is not mentioned as a witness in 1 Cor 15. The position and role of women may perhaps have influenced Paul in his omission of Mary Magdalene's name. If "women are not qualified to be witnesses," then to put their names as witnesses to Christ's appearances would make these lists "illegal." For the early Christians, the list of witnesses "must be invulnerable against the cut and thrust of legal proceedings about the attestation of Christ's resurrection" (E. Stauffer, *op.cit.*, p. 124).

3   *Ibid.*, p. 122.
4   There is, however, a partial parallel to Mt 14:28ff in Jn 21:7–8: "That disciple whom Jesus loved said to Peter, 'It is the Lord!' When Simon Peter heard that it was the Lord, he put on his clothes, for he was stripped for work, and sprang into the sea." Even a partial parallel to Matthew's story in an independent source such as John suggests that the author of our first canonical gospel did not create this Petrine story out of nothing. The scene may have its origin in a post–resurrection appearance: Peter's doubt and the disciples' confession of faith in Jesus as Son of God ("And those in the boat worshipped him, saying, 'Truly you are the Son of God,' [Mt 14:33] would fit in with an Easter setting" [see Reginald H. Fuller, *Matthew*, in *Harper Bible Commentary* (San Francisco, 1988), p. 967]).

Peter. Jesus commands Peter to go "to the sea and cast a hook, and take the first fish that comes up, and when you open its mouth you will find a shekel; take that and give it [to the tax collectors] for me and for yourself" (17:27). Jesus' commands to Peter recall the tradition incorporated in Lk 5:1ff and Jn 21:1–14.

Peter's image in Matthew is not without its "dark" colors, as we have already seen. After the first prediction of the passion, which follows Peter's confession at Ceasarea Philippi, Jesus rebukes Peter even more sternly than in Mark. Only in Matthew's account do we find that Peter is a "stumbling block" (σκάνδαλον) to Jesus (Mt 16:23). Nevertheless, no other gospel gives Peter as prominent a place as Matthew.

Luke underlines the "bright" side of the portrait of Peter given in Mark, and he minimizes its "dark" aspects. There is material in Luke which has no parallels in the other gospels and where Peter is singled out and his leadership and importance conveyed. The first part of this gospel, which deals with Jesus' ministry in Galilee, depicts the miraculous catch of fish (Lk 5:1–11). This is the story of the call of the disciples, and Peter appears as the central figure after Jesus himself. Although Jesus addresses Simon directly—"Do not be afraid; henceforth you will be catching men"—James and John, the sons of Zebedee and Peter's partners, also join him in leaving "everything" in order to follow Jesus (Lk 5:10–11). This Lucan account has some points in common with Jn 21:1–8, which recounts a post-resurrection appearance of Christ. Then in Lk 22:31–34, Jesus converses with Peter:

> "Simon, Simon, behold Satan demanded to have *you*, [ὑμᾶς: plural in Greek] that he might sift *you* [ὑμᾶς: plural] like wheat, but I have prayed for you [here the Greek word is singular, σοῦ, so Peter is addressed] that your faith may not fail; and when you have turned again strengthen your brethren." And he [Peter] said to him, "Lord, I am ready to go with you to prison and to death." He [Jesus] said, "I tell you, Peter, the cock will not crow this day, until you three times deny that you know me."

This conversation reveals how Luke accentuated the positive in the Markan portrait of Peter and reduced its negative, dark aspect. In the first verse (31), Jesus' words are meant for the whole group of the twelve; Satan demands to have them all, not only Peter. It is significant in this connection that in his account of Peter's confession, Luke does not record Peter's rebuke of Jesus, nor does he include Jesus' rebuke of Peter;

"Get behind me, Satan" (see Lk 9:18–22). In Lk 22:32, Peter is singled out and addressed as the one who will be "converted" and become a rallying point and the source of encouragement for others. This is the prophecy which is fulfilled during the post-resurrection period, in Peter's activities within the first Christian community in Jerusalem, as described in Acts 1–12. This passage, in v. 33, also confirms what we have already learned from Mark about Peter's impetuousness. He is quick to react (Mk 8:22) and quick to commit himself to any action (Lk 22:33).

One additional reference in Luke to Peter, which also has no parallel in the synoptic gospels, appears in the chapter on the resurrection and post-resurrection appearances of Jesus. Only in Luke do we find the explicit statement that the Lord "has appeared [ὤφθη] to Simon" (Lk 24:34).[5] What is given in the very early Christian credal statement, 1 Cor 15:5, is confirmed in this gospel. Peter was the first to whom the Risen Lord manifested himself.

Luke portrays Peter in a very favorable light. This is particularly significant because Luke writes to predominantly gentile Christians. He writes to the "most excellent Theophilus," so that he "may know the truth" concerning Jesus and his ministry. And Luke cannot write his narrative, the history of Jesus and his church, without telling the gentile Christians what he knew and had learned about Peter and his relationship with Jesus, as well as about Peter's role in the Jerusalem community. In Luke, therefore, Simon Peter with the Twelve serves as "the bridge between the historical Jesus and the church."[6]

5 Some scholars assert, on the basis of the rendering in *Codex Bezae* of Lk 24:34, that the two men on the way to Emmaus were Cleopas and the Apostle Peter. In *Codex Bezae* we have λέγοντες instead of λέγοντας. As a result of this change, the verses of Lk 24:33–34 are translated as follows: "They found the Eleven and their followers gathered together, and they said: 'the Lord is truly risen and has been seen by Simon'" (J. H. Crehan, "St Peter's Journey to Emmaus," *The Catholic Biblical Quarterly* 15 [1953] 421). This has been regarded as an indication that this announcement was made by Cleopas (see R. Annad, "He was seen of Cephas," *Scottish Journal of Theology* 11 [1958] 180).

    If Peter was with Cleopas, this would be in conflict with the later statement that when they returned to Jerusalem they found "the eleven." Judas, because of his apostasy, could not be numbered among these eleven apostles. Thus the statement seems to exclude the possibility that Peter was with Cleopas. And "they" who said, "the Lord is risen indeed, and has appeared to Simon" does not refer to the "two of them" on the road to Emmaus, but to those whom they found on their return to Jerusalem. It is possible, but in this case not probable, that "the eleven" does not indicate the exact number, but the apostles as one unit, one body.

6 Brown, Donfried, Reumann, *op.cit.,* pp. 127–8.

In the fourth gospel, however, Peter is not presented as πρῶτος, the first disciple to be called. Andrew, Simon Peter's brother, is called first (Jn 1:39–40). The other who is with Andrew is not named. John evidently does not use the Markan narrative of the call of the pair of brothers (Mk 1:16–20). It is also Andrew who acknowledges Jesus as the Messiah, and who introduces Simon to Jesus. Yet that title, "the rock," is not given to Andrew but to his brother Simon (Jn 1:41–42). We have in John an account of Peter's confession which follows the general pattern of the confession narrated in Mark: a request for a sign (Mk 8:11–13; Jn 6:1–5); the discourse on bread (Mk 8:14–21; Jn 6:35–39); Peter's confession (Mk 8:27–30; Jn 6:60–69), and what follows after the confession, the work of Satan, the devil (Mk 8:31–33; Jn 6:70–71).[7] To Jesus' question, whether the twelve would leave him and join many of the disciples who had already withdrawn "and no longer went about with him," Peter responds with his confession: "Lord, to whom shall we go? You have the words of eternal life; and we have believed, and have come to know, that you are the Holy One of God" (Jn 6:67–69). As in Mark, Peter comes forward as the representative of the group and expresses their thoughts. But no special blessing as in Matthew, no special promise, is given to Peter.

In the second part of the fourth gospel (13–21) the Beloved Disciple appears with Peter. We first see him "lying close to the breast of Jesus" (Jn 13:23). He has the "primacy of love." With Jesus the Beloved Disciple enters the high priest's court. Peter is left standing outside. While Peter denies Jesus, the Beloved Disciple remains faithful (Jn 18:15ff). He does not even leave the scene of the crucifixion (Jn 19:25). On the first day of the week, the day of the resurrection, Mary Magdalene goes to Simon Peter and the Beloved Disciple to inform them that the body of the Lord has been taken out of the tomb. While in Luke only Peter runs to the tomb—"stooping and looking in, he saw the linen clothes by themselves; and he went home wondering at what had happened" (Lk 24:12)—in John, Peter and the Beloved Disciple run together. The Beloved Disciple outruns Peter, reaches the tomb first, looks in, goes in, and on the basis of what he sees in the empty tomb, "the napkin, which had been on [Jesus'] head, not lying with the linen clothes but

7 *Ibid.*, p. 64, note 144. This implies that the evangelists, independently of one another, found the pattern in tradition or in sources they received and used.

rolled up in a place by itself" (Jn 20:7), he believes that Jesus has been raised from the dead (Jn 20:8). The Beloved Disciple is the first to believe, even before the Risen Lord makes himself known to his disciples. And when Jesus reveals himself by the Sea of Tiberias, it is the Beloved Disciple who says to Peter, "It is the Lord!" Again he is the first to recognize him.

Who is the Beloved Disciple? He appears only in the Gospel of John, but his identity or name is never revealed. At the end of John, he is identified as the one who bears witness to the tradition incorporated in this Gospel, and as the one who has written it—as its author (Jn 21:24). Irenaeus, at the end of the second century, identifies him as John, the son of Zebedee. But the frequent episodes, scenes and references where the sons of Zebedee are mentioned in Mark and the other two synoptic gospels (Mk 1:19–20; 1:29; 3:17; 5:37; 9:2; 10:35–45; 13:3; 14:3) are not to be found in John. Some modern scholars do not accept that John, the son of Zebedee, is the author of the fourth gospel. Others take the early Christian tradition of John's authorship seriously and suggest that the originator of the tradition is probably John, but that he is not necessarily the author of the gospel. Who wrote the gospel? The question is not resolved, and neither is the mystery of the identity of the Beloved Disciple, who is a real, concrete figure in the Johannine community. His identity remains uncertain, but his image, depicted in John, as a true follower and believer is clearly manifested. He has a "primacy of love, faith, and recognition" in the community, but he is not set over against Peter. There is no conflict between them.

In sum, we note that there is no bias against Peter in the Gospel of John. Peter's misunderstanding of Jesus' act of washing the disciples' feet (Jn 13:6–11), his readiness to act to protect Jesus (Jn 18:10–11), and his impetuousness (Jn 21:7–8) are characteristics that are already depicted in the synoptic gospels. He is not σκάνδαλον in John. The author of the fourth gospel in fact "names Peter more than any other gospel writer does."[8] We have to conclude that, for the fourth evangelist as well, the

8   P. Parker, "John and Mark," *Journal of Biblical Literature* 79:2 (1960) 101. The author of this article proposes John Mark as the author of the fourth Gospel. This theory influences his evaluation of the place of Peter in the second Gospel. He states that this gospel narrative gives us less material about Peter than either Matthew, Luke, or John. According to second century tradition, Mark is Peter's interpreter. In Parker's view, "the unnamed disciple constantly acts as interpreter for Peter...Always he opens the way for Peter, explains, interprets for him" (p.

story of Jesus cannot be complete without the story of Peter.

In the last scene of John's gospel we have an interchange between Jesus and Peter (Jn 21:15–17). This is a truly Petrine passage. Three times Jesus asks Peter, "Do you love me?"; and three times Peter answers that he loves the Lord. After each response the Risen Christ commissions Peter to feed (βόσκειν) and tend (ποιμαίνειν) his, i.e., Christ's, flock. Clearly, after the resurrection, Peter is reestablished and given the role of shepherd. The verb ποιμαίνειν conveys more than βόσκειν. In a figurative sense, ποιμαίνειν points to the duties and responsibilities of church leaders—protecting, governing, leading, and caring for the people under their charge. Βόσκειν, on the other hand, points to the shepherd's activities of feeding or tending. Jn 21:15–17 does not imply that Peter is given the position of "primacy" or "superiority" over other Christian shepherds—only that his relationship with Jesus is restored.

While the passion story tells of Peter's failure, this post-resurrection narrative recounts the restoration and "the growth of Peter." Peter became the leader of the earliest Christian community. On the day of Pentecost, he addresses the people (Acts 2), exercising his power of binding and loosing (Acts 5). The sick were carried out into the streets, "that as Peter came by at least his shadow might fall on some of them" (Acts 5:15) and heal them. Before the high priest, who asked the apostles not to teach in Jesus' name, "Peter and the apostles answered, 'We must obey God rather than men'" (Acts 5:29). Thus Peter overcame the temptation to which he had succumbed during the ministry of Christ,

102). On the other hand, Vincent Taylor (*The Gospel According to St Mark* [London, 1955], p. 168) makes the following comment: "Proportionately to its size, Mk mentions the apostle more frequently than Mt or Lk,…the vividness with which the personality of the apostle is presented in Mk is characteristic of the Gospel and is in harmony with the Papias tradition." Taylor's conclusion seems to be justified by a study of all the references to Peter in the synoptic gospels. In Mk we have Petrine stories (1:29–31; 4:35–41) which probably come from Peter himself. In the Gospel of Mark, the story of the healing of Simon's mother-in-law is described in forty-four words in Greek; but the first evangelist, in his much longer Gospel, presents the story in only thirty words. Mark's account is not only longer but much more graphic than either Matthew's or Luke's, where the narrative is presented in thirty-eight words. To this we may add that Mk 1:29–31 is part of a longer narrative, which describes the first day of the Lord, the manifestation of the Day of the Lord (1:21–34). This passage describes Jesus, entering the synagogue, His teaching and healing the sick, and, at the end of the day, "that evening, at sundown," healing and casting out demons. On this first day Jesus "entered the house of Simon and Andrew…"

when he had been rebuked for being not on the side of God but of men (Mt 16:23). Peter worked as a missionary in Judaea, Galilee and Samaria. He was called the Apostle of the Circumcised, the missionary among the Jews. "Feed my lambs, shepherd my sheep" may point primarily to this vocation as a missionary to the Jews.[9] As a shepherd, his devotion to Christ's flock must be total. "The good shepherd lays down his life for the sheep" (Jn 10:11). And after Jesus says to Peter for the third time, "Feed my sheep," he indicates by which kind of death Peter would glorify God (Jn 21:18–19).[10]

II

The confession of Peter is followed immediately by the often-quoted blessing and promise of Jesus to Peter:

> Blessed are you, Simon Bar-Jona, for flesh and blood has not revealed this to you, but my Father who is in heaven. And I tell you, you are Peter (Πέτρος), and on this rock (πέτρα) I will build my church (ἐκκλησίαν), and the powers of death shall not prevail against it. I will give you the keys of the Kingdom of heaven, and whatever you bind on earth shall be bound in heaven and whatever you loose on earth shall be loosed in heaven. (Mt 16:17–19)

Among the gospel passages that have been used to support the claim of the primacy of Peter and the Church of Rome, these verses from Matthew's gospel have played the most significant role. Our discussion will therefore concentrate on this passage.

This crucial account is found only in Matthew. Its omission in Mark and Luke was already the subject of discussion in the early church.

9 A Fridrichsen, *The Apostle and His Message, Uppsala Universitets Arsskrift* 3 (1947) 18, note 12. He sees "vestiges" in Jn 21:15ff of Peter's call to be apostle to the Circumcised; and he adds that Mt 16:19 may be taken as a variant of the same tradition as Jn 21:15–17. See also H. Mosbech, "*Apostolos* in the New Testament," in *Studia Theologica* 2 (1950) 182.

10 The New Testament contains no explicit statement that Peter suffered martyrdom in Rome. John's hint in 21:18–19 is supported by early testimony, dating ca. 100 A.D.: "Let us take the noble examples of our own generation. By reason of rivalry and envy the greatest and most righteous pillars [of the Church] were persecuted, and battled to the death. Let us set before our eyes the noble apostles: Peter [and] Paul..." (*I Clement* 5:1–6). Ignatius in *Romans* 4:3 writes: "Pray Christ for me that by these means I may become God's sacrifice. I do not give you orders like Peter and Paul. They were apostles: I am a convict. They were at liberty: I am still a slave. But if I suffer, I shall be emancipated by Jesus Christ; and united to him, I shall rise to freedom" (See Cyril C. Richardson, ed., *Early Christian Fathers* [Philadelphia, 1953], pp. 45–46, 104).

Eusebius, for example, tried to explain that Mark,

the friend and follower of Peter, whose teaching he repeats, does not record that Jesus said anything in reply to Peter's confession…probably because Peter did not speak of it in his teaching and wished it passed over in silence. But Peter published to all men his denial, hence Mark records it. This is a proof that Peter was far removed from self-love, and was of a truth-loving disposition.[11]

This solution, based upon the humbleness and modesty of Peter, has satisfied very few indeed. Attributing the existence of these verses to a particularly favorable attitude toward Peter in Matthew, and their omissions to a bias against the first apostle of Jesus in Mark and Luke, cannot be supported by the evidence from the gospels themselves. As we have already seen, it is difficult to detect any hostile inclination against Peter in any of the four gospels or in the Book of Acts.

Certain modern scholars have explained the omission of this blessing (Mt 16:17–19) at Caesarea Philipppi in Mark's and Luke's accounts of the confession of Peter as an indication that it may have occurred in another context during the ministry of Jesus. They do not question the historical fact of Peter's confession, but they doubt that the passage belongs here. Oscar Cullmann has proposed the passion narrative, more precisely the Last Supper, as the context for Mt 16:17–19.[12] On the other hand, Johannes Munck thinks that Cullmann "has not succeeded in showing convincingly that the words were originally part of the story of the Passion." Munck takes Lk 24:34 and 1 Cor 15:5, Christ's appearance to Peter after the resurrection, as its "outer framework."[13] This reflects the prevailing hypothesis among New Testament scholars that the passage should be transferred to the post-resurrection period. Some of Christ's revelations after the resurrection are "church-founding" appearances, "which provide for preaching, baptizing, forgiving sins and other means of beginning, enlarging, and continuing the Christian community," and this context may be "more appropriate" for Mt 16:18 than its present setting.[14] This is the assessment by both Protestant and Roman Catholic scholars. "The

---

11 *Dem. Evang.* 3, 5, given in Harold Smith, *Ante-Nicene Exegesis of the Gospels*, v. III (London, 1925), pp. 149–150.
12 O. Cullmann, *Peter* (Philadelphia, 1953), pp. 170ff.
13 J. Munck, *Paul and the Salvation of Mankind* (London, 1959), p. 63.
14 Brown, Donfried, and Reumann, *op. cit.*, p. 35, note 78, and p. 92. On the nature of the post-resurrection appearances, see our book *The First Day of the New Creation* (*The Resurrection and Christian Faith*) (Crestwood, NY: St Vladimir's Seminary Press, 1982), pp. 88ff.

original context of vv. 17–19 may have been the Easter appearance of Christ to Peter," summarizes John P. Meier, a Roman Catholic specialist in Matthew's gospel.[15]

By moving Mt 16:17–19 from the context of Peter's confession to the post-resurrection period, modern scholars do not necessarily weaken the claim of the Roman primacy, but quite the opposite. They may be strengthening it, for in this case these words are not immediately connected to Jesus' harsh rebuke of Peter as σκάνδαλον (Mt 16:23). Those who accept the present setting of Mt 16:17–19 as the original, and who reject placing these verses either within the Passion event or the appearance and pronouncement of the Risen Lord, see them as being fulfilled in the first eucharistic gathering in Jerusalem, at which Peter was presiding.[16]

The context of Mt 16:17–19—whatever it may be—does not undermine the authenticity of these verses. That they are found only in Matthew does not mean that they are a free creation of the evangelist or of the church for which he writes. The Gospel of Matthew was most probably composed in Syria and addressed to the Church in Antioch, which particularly revered the Apostle Peter. Certain traditions about Peter which are not recorded in Mark or Luke were preserved and shaped in the Aramaic-speaking community and incorporated into the content of the confession of Peter by the first evangelist. In some other churches, by contrast, the apostle John probably had more prestige than any other of Jesus' disciples. If the Gospel of Matthew was written for a Jewish Christian church which was ready to widen its missionary activities among the gentiles, then it would be important to remind this Christian community that the leader of Jewish Christianity was also open to the gentile mission (Acts 10). He had been given the power of binding and loosing. This may be the reason for the collection and use of special Petrine traditions,[17] which Matthew found in his sources.

15 On Matthew (Wilmington, DE: Michael Glazier, 1980), p. 179.

16 Fr. Nicolas Afanassieff, in his essay, "L'Apôtre Pierre et l'Evêque de Rome," in Théologie 26 (1955), pp. 3–35, looks upon this problem from a completely different perspective. He sees it in terms of eucharistic ecclesiology, and he refuses to ascribe these verses either to the narrative of the Passion or to the pronouncement of the Risen Lord (pp. 13–17). And Joseph Ludwig ("Die Primatworte Mt 16:18–19 in der Altkirchlichen Exegese," in Neutestamentliche Abhandlungen XIX:4 [1952] 6) writes as follows: "Glaube, Kirche, Opfer: das ist der innerste Kreis des Lebens Jesu, und wenn eins seinter Worte 'en Sitz im Leben' hat, dann Mt 16:18–19."

17 "The very favorable view of Peter in Matthew may possibly be related to the Jewish Christian

It has long been noticed that Mt 16:17–19 has a Palestinian, Aramaic background. The form of Jesus' reply to Peter's confession appears Hebraistic.[18] There are parallels to the Matthean text in the Qumran literature.[19] The use of semitisms such as "gates of Hades," "flesh and blood," "bind and loose," and semitic parallelism again indicates an Aramaic environment. John Breck, in his forthcoming book, writes of the parallel structure of Mt 16:17–19, that each of these three verses "represents a strophe of three lines, beginning with a thematic statement (A), followed by antithetical qualifying phrases (B–B')." To illustrate, let us take v. 17:

A: "Blessed are you, Simon Bar-Jonah,

B: for flesh and blood did not reveal (this) to you,

B': but my Father (who is) in the heavens."

The same structure (A–B–B') characterizes the other two verses, 18 and 19. This would support their Semitic background. We cannot define with any assurance the exact words which Jesus addressed to Peter: his words, inspired by, developed, and understood under the influence of the Holy Spirit, have their own history in the living Body of Christ. Both the community that remembered and considered them precious, as well as the evangelist who placed them in his gospel, contributed to their final shape. But we can say with a certain confidence that these recorded verses contain nothing that would contradict Jesus' teaching and work as they are presented in the Gospels. We accept them as the authentic words of Christ.

III

Jesus told Simon that a weak, mortal man, "flesh and blood," could not perceive who he was. For this insight the disciple needed a special revelation by God. He conferred upon Simon Bar-Jonah the title Peter, and promised that he would build his church upon him. "You are Peter

---

background of the Matthean community" (Brown, Donfried, and Reumann, *op. cit.,* p. 75).

18 A. Edersheim, *The Life and Times of Jesus the Messiah,* v. II (London, 1896), p. 81.

19 Otto Bentz, "Felsenmann und Felsen-Femeinde (Eine Parallele zu Mt 16:17–19 in den Qumranpsalmen)," in *Zeitschrift für die Neutestamentliche Wissenschaft* 48 (1957) 49–77. He considers Mt 16:17–19 against the background of the group of images of the holy building in Qumran Thanksgiving Hymns (*Hodayot*). On the basis of this comparison, he comes to the conclusion that Jesus intended to build the church which would carry on his teachings and his work (p. 76).

(Πέτρος), and on this rock (πέτρᾳ) I will build my church (μου τὴν ἐκκλησίαν)." These words are spoken in Aramaic, in which Cephas stands both for Πέτρος and πέτρᾳ. The translation of the word Cephas into Greek Πέτρος "confirms the fact that the word is not a proper name," writes Cullmann; proper names are not translated, "and if we must translate them, then in order to preserve the original impact of the word Cephas we should instead of 'Simon Peter' have 'Simon Rock.'"[20] Only at the end of the second century was Πέτρος used as a proper name, and as a Christian name it first appears in Tertullian.[21]

The confession of Peter, therefore, cannot be separated from Peter himself. Πέτρα or rock does not simply refer to Peter's faith but also to Peter personally. There is a formal and real identity between Πέτρος and πέτρᾳ.[22] Jesus will build the church upon Cephas.

The word ἐκκλησία, very common in the letters of Paul, is not used in the gospels except in Mt 16:18 and 18:17. The term is primarily used in the New Testament to mean a local church. The introductions to some of the Pauline letters are instructive in this regard. The recipient of 1 Corinthians, for instance, is "the Church of God which is in Corinth" (1 Cor 1:2). The church at Corinth is a local church, yet it is the Catholic Church. It is not a part of the universal Church but is in itself "the universal church," in the sense of Ignatius' words, "where Jesus Christ is, there is the Catholic Church,"[23] or as Irenaeus says, "where the church is, there is to be found the Holy Spirit and all grace."[24] Consequently, the church in its fullness is present in a limited locality. The term ἐκκλησία in the New Testament primarily means a local church.[25]

In the letters of Paul to the Ephesians and Colossians (1:18) and in a few other places in the New Testament, however, the term ἐκκλησία does refer to the universal church. An example of this may be Jesus' promise to Peter. "It seems obvious that, when our Lord says 'On this rock I will build my church,' he has in mind not a particular local church

20 O. Cullmann, *op. cit.,* p. 19, and, by the same author, see "Peter" in *TDNT,* v. VI, p. 100.
21 See John Lowe, *Saint Peter* (New York, 1956), pp. 7–8.
22 O. Cullmann, "Peter," in *TDNT,* v. VI, p. 98.
23 *Smyr.* 8, 2.
24 PG 7, col. 966, as quoted by Y. Congar, *The Mystery of the Church* (London, 1960), p. 40.
25 Y. Campbell, "The Origin and Meaning of the Christian Use of the Word *ekklesia,*" *Journal of Theological Studies* 49 (1984) 139.

(for local churches did not yet exist) but the Catholic Church as a whole," argues a modern Orthodox theologian and bishop.[26] The church in Jerusalem, with Peter at the head of the first gathering of the new people of God, was not a part of Christ's universal church, but its full realization and manifestation. This catholic church transcends a particular locality, and it will also be fully realized in other local churches founded by the followers of Christ.

The local churches are united with one another. They belong to Christ, and the unity of the church is to be found "in Jesus," in him who, in the vision of the seer on the island of Patmos, holds the seven stars and is seen in the midst of seven golden lampstands (Rev 1:12ff). The seven lampstands represent the seven local churches in Asia Minor, and each one of them "is the church universal in all its fulness."[27]

The Messiah has come. He is Jesus of Nazareth. He appointed twelve disciples. The Messiah is not alone, for he creates his own community. The twelve represent Israel, who are asked to follow him. His coming, as well as his call of the twelve, points to Jesus' self-understanding and to his intention to build "my church," which would carry on his work. This is also suggested by the very title which Christ applied to himself—Son of Man. Taken from Dan 7:13 and 1 Enoch, this name embraces both the communal and individual aspects of Jesus' work, and points to the foundation of the eschatological community. "The Son of Man" is the messianic title which expresses the role of the Messiah in his humiliation and suffering, as well as in his exaltation and divine sovereignty. Accordingly, Jesus' reply to Peter in Mt 16:17–19 cannot be considered in isolation. Not only are we certain that "Mt 16:18 does not stand alone," writes K. L. Schmidt,

> but [we] also realize...that this conception of the complex of ideas (Jesus, Messiah, Son of Man, Disciples, Community, Lord's Supper) leads directly to the Pauline and sub-Pauline doctrines of the ἐκκλησία, which on the one hand is "from above" and on the other is "the Body of Christ," just as Christ is at the same time highly exalted and present in the midst of the community. The question whether Jesus himself founded the church is really the question

---

26　Archbishop Basil (Krivoshein) of Brussels, "Catholicity and the Structures of the Church," *St Vladimir's Theological Quarterly* 17 (1973) 44.
27　G. B. Caird, *The Revelation of St John the Divine* (New York, 1966), pp. 24–25. See also his commentary on Rev 22.

concerning his Messiahship.[28]

There is no consensus among New Testament scholars regarding what Aramaic expression is translated as ἐκκλησία in Mt 16:18. There are Hebrew terms for the community of God's people: *gahal,* which may be translated as "the assembly of Israel," or *eda,* "assembly," used by the Qumran community to designate the gathering of the chosen ones. "In Aramaic, one could say either *dta* or *kenishta* or even *gehala.*"[29] It is worth noting that although the Septuagint in a number of cases translated the Hebrew words *gahal* or *eda* as ἐκκλησία, these terms are also translated by the word συναγωγή, "meeting," "the place of gathering," which corresponds to the Aramaic work *kenishta,* "house of prayer."[30] Non-Christian Jews used συναγωγή for the local gathering in diaspora, but Jewish Christians in the Hellenistic world preferred the term ἐκκλησία, in order to convey both the local and the universal character of their gathering.

Which term did Jesus use to designate his community? We should eliminate the Qumran concept of *eda,* for the simple reason that this term, as it is used in this community, implies its exclusive character. "The little flock" (Lk 12:32) is not an exclusive group. Jesus proclaimed the Kingdom of God and sent out the twelve to preach and gave them authority to cast out demons. This community of the "end-time" started with the election and call of the twelve and was implied in Jesus' promise to Peter: "I will build my church." This leaves the Aramaic terms *gehala* and *kenishta.* It is most likely that he used *gehala* to indicate the character of his community, as "people set apart for God's special service" in their universal mission.

28 K. L. Schmidt, "The Church," in *TDNT,* v. III, pp. 521ff. H. Charlesworth, ed. of *Old Testament Pseudepigrapha* and author of *Jesus within Judaism* (*New Light from Exciting Archaeological Discoveries*) (New York: Doubleday, 1988), writes that in choosing this number Jesus reveals a specific intent. "Twelve" is the number of the twelve sons of Jacob, the number that represents Israel: "Is there some self-understanding behind Jesus' apparent desire to have twelve special men follow him? Is he by this act not symbolically representing a belief that the end of time is now becoming a present reality? Since he is the one who chose the twelve, is he not exhibiting some perception of playing in the eschatological restoration of Israel? It is unwise, indeed uninformed, to follow the lead of some New Testament scholars who denounce any possibility of recovering Jesus' self-understanding; and it may no longer be wise to reject the possibility that he had some 'messianic' self-understanding" (p. 138).
29 See Xavier Léon-Dufour, *Dictionary of the New Testament* (San Francisco: Harper and Row, 1980), pp. 134–135.
30 *Ibid.,* p. 391.

Kenishta, as we have seen, stands for a local Jewish community.

In the church built on Rock, Peter was promised "the keys of the kingdom of heaven," which are the symbol of the authority of binding and loosing. By the time of Jesus these two terms, mentioned in rabbinic sources, also had the additional meanings of forbidding and permitting. The duty of the teachers of Israel was to specify which works or activities were permitted and which were forbidden on the Sabbath Day.[31] Jesus promises that whatever Peter forbids on earth shall be forbidden in heaven. The meaning of this verse (Mt 16:19) becomes clear if we see it in the light of Jn 14:16f and 26 ("But the Counselor, the Holy Spirit, whom the Father will send in my name, he will teach you all things, and bring to your remembrance all that I have said to you"). Then "it is the church on earth carrying out heaven's decisions communicated by the Spirit, and not heaven ratifying the church's decision," comments W. F. Albright.[32]

This power of binding and loosing is not given only to Peter but also to the other apostles (Mt 18:18). The leaders of the church, like the teachers of Israel, are granted the authority to interpret scriptures and to find answers to the problems which confront the community of their time. The apostolic council at Jerusalem (Acts 15) can serve as a telling example of how the authority was exercised and should be exercised in the church. The problem that confronted the church was whether or not to impose circumcision on the gentiles. This was an essentially religious problem with cultural overtones. Although Jesus did not say anything explicit about the issue, the apostles and the missionaries who gathered together under the leadership of James rightly interpreted the gospel of Jesus and came to the decision which represented a turning point in the history of the church. The spread of the Christian message throughout the gentile world, "to make disciples of all nations," was now guaranteed.

31 David Bivin and Roy Blizzard, Jr, *Understanding the Difficult Words of Jesus (New Insights from a Hebrew Perspective)* (Austin, TX, 1984). Work in itself, according to the Rabbis, "is not necessarily an activity which causes physical or mental fatigue. Study is allowed on the Sabbath," but "the mere striking of a match, just once, is a desecration of the Sabbath because it involves creation." Work is defined "as any activity involving the production, creation, or transformation of an object" (p. 145). Undoubtedly there is an arbitrary element in this definition.

32 On Mt 16:19, see W. F. Albright and C. S. Mann, *Matthew, Anchor Bible* (Garden City, NY, 1971).

The power promised to Peter was now exercised not only by Peter, but also by Paul, and above all by James, who was at this time the "Rock" upon which the church was built. The power given to Peter is the same power that is granted to the other members of the group of the twelve (Mt 18:18). Some exegetes have tried to distinguish between "teaching authority" in Mt 16 and "the power to excommunicate" in Mt 18. They distinguish the power given to Peter with the promise of "the keys of the Kingdom" (16:19) from the power granted to the others (18:18). Peter, they argue, has the authority "to make decisions for the universal church ('my church')," while the others use the given power for "disciplinary actions by the local communities."[33] These interpreters overstress the omission of the phrase "keys of the Kingdom" in 18:18 and neglect the parallel structure of Mt 16:19, where the "binding" and "loosing" help us to understand what is meant by the authority of "the keys of the Kingdom."

This distinction between teaching and pastoral authority is too sharp and cannot be supported by the evidence from the New Testament. The universal church and the local church, as we have seen, cannot be separated. Neither can we draw a clear line between teaching and pastoral authority. All the apostles have both. James, the brother of the Lord, exercised both "doctrinal" and "pastoral" authority at the council. By giving its consent to the decision of the Jerusalem church leaders, the whole church participated in the power of binding and loosing. Nothing may be done in the church without the participation of the faithful. For the community of believers, which Paul designated as "Christ" (1 Cor 12:12), is the community that preaches, teaches, and mediates Christ to the world. Paul, for instance, who has "already pronounced judgment in the name of the Lord Jesus" upon a Corinthian Christian who was living with his father's wife, asks the members, when they are assembled as the church, to excommunicate the transgressor from their midst (1 Cor 5:1–5). Paul appeals to the whole community to make its decision and support its leader.

The authority of "binding" and "loosing," therefore, is not limited to the twelve, but goes beyond this group. J. C. O'Neill relates 2 Cor 2:10f—"Any one whom you forgive, I also forgive. What I have forgiven, if I have forgiven anything, has been for your sake in the presence

33 J. P. Meier, *op. cit.*, p. 183.

of Christ"—to the "binding" and "loosing" in Mt 16:19.[34]

Modern exegesis of Mt 16 appears to be less and less apologetic. Yet it reveals more and not less about Peter and his "special" role in the New Testament church. He alone is addressed by Jesus, "You are Cephas," and to him personally the promise is given. Why, then, are there so many controversies regarding the role and the place of Peter in the church?

IV

The promises made to Peter (Mt 16:17–19, Lk 22:32, Jn 21:15–17) have been taken by the Church of Rome as the basis for the doctrine of the unique status of Peter among the twelve. According to this doctrine, Peter had the primacy, more power and authority than any other disciple. By the fourth century, the claim is made that the Bishop of Rome, as the successor to Peter, that is, the successor to his apostolic power and authority, enjoys particular privilege. If Peter was above all others, so the Bishop of Rome, as his successor, is above all other local church bishops and leaders; Rome has claimed authority over the universal church. These are the reasons for the disputes between Christians of the East and the West. These disputes raise two questions regarding Peter's role and position in the New Testament: first, did Peter have the primacy; and second, did he have successors?

During Christ's public ministry Peter is the leader of the twelve, but he is not above the other apostles. He does not have power and authority above them. When Jesus humbled himself by washing the feet of his disciples, he also showed that the twelve were equal.[35] Peter is presented in the gospels as the leading disciple, with all his weaknesses, but never as a "super-apostle."

After the resurrection and ascension of Christ, however, it would be inaccurate to describe Peter as holding a position of primacy in the Apostolic Church. At a certain time, Peter's leadership over the Church in Jerusalem terminated, and James, the brother of the Lord, appeared as the new leader of that church. We cannot say just when this occurred, perhaps after the death of James the brother of John (Acts 12). The Book

---

34 J. C. O'Neill, *Messiah (Six Lectures on the Ministry of Jesus)* (Cambridge: Cochrane Press, 1980), as quoted by E. P. Sanders, *Jesus and Judaism* (Philadelphia: Fortress Press, 1985), p. 105.

35 Bishop Cassian, "Saint Pierre et l'église dans le Nouveau Testament (le problème de la primauté)," *Istina* 3 (1955) 289.

of Acts, as well as the Epistle to the Galatians, imply the change without indicating when it took place. When Paul went to Jerusalem for the first time after his conversion, he went there in order to visit Cephas, and he stayed with Peter fifteen days (Gal 1:18). Peter, at this time, was the head of the community. Fourteen years later, Paul again went to Jerusalem, not drawn by his own desire but by "revelation" (Gal 2:1–2), and he mentioned three pillars, the first of whom was James (Gal 2:9). At the first Apostolic Council, described in Acts 15, it was James who played the role of the leader. According to Acts 21:8, when Paul again found himself in Jerusalem, James is the only one mentioned by name.

The evidence points to the preeminence of the Church in Jerusalem and her leaders, rather than to the primacy of any Apostle, either Peter or James. Jerusalem, God's chosen city, is the place of Christ's crucifixion and resurrection. At the time of Pentecost, the Gospel is proclaimed to Israel in this city, to the Jews from Palestine, as well as to those from the Diaspora. It is the center of missionary activity to Israel; and Paul, by his visits to Jerusalem, demonstrates the significance of the gentile mission for the salvation of both Jews and Greeks. Still, neither these visits by Paul nor his collection for the poor in Jerusalem suggest that Jerusalem exercises authority over the young churches, and the church leaders in the city do not try to bring these churches under their supervision. It is doubtful that even Gal 2:12 indicates this. When other local churches come into existence, Jerusalem has no primacy over them. The primacy of honor which the Holy City holds among other churches is derived from the events of salvation which took place there, as well as from its being the first ἐκκλησία in Christ— not from power over other churches, which Jerusalem does not possess.

What could Peter, the leader of the twelve, transmit to his successors? The twelve held a special position among the New Testament apostles. Barnabas and Paul were also apostles. "But while Paul claimed parity with the Twelve in the matter of apostleship," T. W. Manson observes, "he did not claim to be one of the Twelve. Nor did anybody else."[36] The twelve, who received the Gospel for us from Christ, had a special status in the early community. The office of the twelve was one of service, not of privilege. What privilege there was came from the fact that the apostle was directly called by Christ.[37] In the

36 T. W. Manson, *The Church's Ministry* (Philadelphia, 1950), pp. 53–54.
37 H. Mosbech, *op. cit.*, p. 177.

full sense of the word, the twelve became apostles with the resurrection of Christ.[38] They were witnesses to Jesus' public ministry, to his resurrection, and they were therefore the first Christian missionaries.[39] In authority and power they were equal; there were no degrees of power in the circle of the twelve, although there were "degrees of intimacy,"[40] or what we may call "degrees of honor."[41] When a dispute arose as to "who is the greatest in the Kingdom of Heaven" (Mt 18:2), Christ called a child, put it in the midst of his disciples, and spoke to them about littleness, not importance. When the mother of the sons of Zebedee asked for special places for her two sons, Jesus pointed to their suffering and martyrdom. During the Last Supper, when the disciples again harbored thoughts of greatness, Jesus exhorted them to service. Instead of "degrees of greatness," Christ said that humility, suffering and service would be their future lot.

The number of the twelve could neither be reduced nor increased. They are the twelve, and to them Christ promised that they would sit on thrones and would judge the twelve tribes of Israel (Lk 22:30, Rev 3:21). When James, the brother of John, was killed (Acts 12:1), no one took his place among the twelve. But after Judas' death, his office was taken by another disciple of Jesus. It was Judas' apostasy, not his death, that forced the selection of a new apostle.[42] With the choice of Matthias to fill the vacancy, God Himself, not the community, created a new apostle. The community selected two persons who fulfilled the requirement, namely,

38 Karl Heinrich Rengstorf writes that "the act of the risen Lord...was the renewal of the commission of the disciples in their definitive institution as ἀπόστολοι," (Mt 28:16ff, Lk 24:48f, Acts 1:8, "ἀπόστολος" in *TDNT*, v. I, p. 430).

39 *Ibid.*, p. 44. "The missionary element fundamentally differentiates the New Testament apostleship from the Jewish *shaliah* institution."

40 T. W. Manson, *op. cit.*, p. 51.

41 Honors in the Kingdom are not equal, writes Chrysostom. The three disciples were preeminent above the rest, "and among these three again there was a great difference. For this is a very exact method observed by God even to the last. Hence 'one star differeth from another star in glory,' [1 Cor 15:41] it says. And yet all were Apostles and all are to sit on twelve thrones, and all left their goods, and all companied with him; still it was the three he took...and he sets Peter before them, when he says, 'Lovest thou me more than these?' [Jn 21:15]. And John too was loved even above the rest" (*Hom XXXI on Romans*, in NPNF, v. XI, p. 557). From this quotation and from what immediately follows, it is clear that we have here not primacy of power or of authority, but preeminence of honor.

42 C. H. Dodd, in *According to the Scriptures* (New York, 1953), pp. 58–59, note 1, formulates this problem as follows: "The mere death of an apostle need not have created a vacancy: *en te palingenesia* he would be there to take his throne, but apostasy is a different matter."

"who have accompanied us during all the time that the Lord Jesus went in and out among us, beginning from the baptism of John until the day when he was taken up from us—one of these men must become with us a witness to his resurrection" (Acts 1:21–22), and it was God who appointed Matthias. The lots which they cast stand for God's choice.[43]

The apostles are presented in the New Testament as a group with a special position. The early history of the church also confirms their unique status. In his essay, which draws evidence from Irenaeus and Eusebius, C. H. Turner shows that the bishops who carry on the apostolic succession in Antioch, Jerusalem, Alexandria, and Rome are distinguished from the apostles who founded these churches.[44] A line is drawn between the apostles as the founders, and the bishops as their successors. In Rome, for example, Linus is "first after Paul and Peter." It does not say that he is "second." Clement, coming after Linus and Anencietus, is "in the third place from the apostles." At Antioch, Ignatius is "second in the Petrine succession" in this city. "In whatever sense the bishops are successors of the apostles," writes Turner, "the office of the apostles is not identified with the office of their successors...Neither in Irenaeus nor in Eusebius are the Apostles counted as units in the episcopal list."[45]

The special status of those who knew Christ at the time of his ministry, who were with him, who were witnesses to his resurrection, cannot be transmitted to their successors. The post-resurrection appearances were "revelatory events," and in them Christ made himself known. Some of the events are characterized as "church-founding"—without

43 In *Hom. III on the Acts of the Apostles*, and in connection with Matthias' choice, Chrysostom comments that Peter did not make appointments. He acted as "expositor, not as preceptor." Peter, writes Chrysostom, "does everything with the common consent, nothing imperiously" (NPNF, v. 11, pp. 18–19).

44 C. H. Turner, "Apostolic Succession," in H. B. Swete, *Essays on the Early History of the Church and the Ministry* (London, 1918), pp. 95–142.

45 *Ibid.*, p. 140. See Sergius Bulgakov, "The Hierarchy and the Sacraments," in *The Ministry and the Sacraments*, ed. by R. Dunkerley (New York, 1937), pp. 95–123. He states that "the Church is called Apostolic, not only because it has the apostolic succession of episcopal ordination, but also with reference to the whole fullness of apostolic tradition. And apostolic succession in this latter sense applies to the *whole* church and not only to the hierarchy...the apostles founded the Christian hierarchy not only in their capacity of first bishops but in all the fullness of their apostleship, which cannot as such be transferred to anybody (p. 98). All gifts were given to the whole church, and "the church was able to differentiate various organs for the fulfillment of specific functions and to establish hierarchy...hierarchy exists in and for the church, and is not over it; it is an organ of the church, endowed with special powers" (p. 103).

them there would be no church. It has been recognized that the disciples' experience of the risen Christ cannot be compared with any visionary spiritual experience, with any form of mysticism. For Karl Rahner, the post-resurrection experiences of Christ's disciples are "strictly *sui generis*,"[46] and they belong to the very origin of the church. No one can succeed to the unique status promised to the twelve (Lk 22:30). The apostles cannot hand over their places in a kingdom appointed to them, nor can Peter transfer his role as the rock of the first Church in Christ. Only the church as a whole succeeds to these apostolic privileges. The apostles' successor is the apostolic church, which possesses the fullness of apostolic tradition and with which Christ identifies himself (Acts 9:4). Every bishop in the apostolic church who occupies the place which Peter occupied at the eucharistic gathering, and who performs the pastoral duties which Peter performed, is the successor to the apostle.[47] But no bishop can succeed to Peter's unique place as a member of the twelve, as the first witness of the resurrection, and as the first head of the first assembly in Christ. Both the New Testament and the early history of the church are in full agreement on this point.

V

From the New Testament perspective, there is not, and there cannot be, a successor to Peter or to any of the twelve disciples. What is given to Peter personally cannot be transferred to anyone else. There was no leader in the primitive Christian community who enjoyed the primacy, and no church had primacy over other local churches. If we must name the apostle who contributed more than any other to the rise and importance of the Roman see, then this apostle was not Peter but Paul.

Peter remained faithful to Jerusalem. His particular concern was for the Jewish Christians in the Holy City (Gal 2:11ff). Paul, the apostle to the gentiles, came to Jerusalem three years after his conversion to learn about Jesus from Peter (Gal 1:18). He knew about Peter's standing and importance in the church of Jerusalem, he desired to know as much as possible about Jesus of Nazareth, and he was aware that this could not be achieved

46 See Gerald O'Collins, *Interpreting the Resurrection* (*Examining the Major Problems in the Stories of Jesus' Resurrection*) (New York: Paulist Press, 1988), pp. 5–21.
47 John Meyendorff, *Orthodoxy and Catholicity* (New York: Sheed and Ward, 1966), pp. 8-13.

without Peter. There is no detectable bias against Peter in the Pauline epistles. In 1 Corinthians, we find a reference to Cephas' party, probably a group of people in Corinth adhering to Peter; Paul criticizes the sectarian spirit of this faction, but not Peter personally. If there was any teaching concerning Peter's supremacy, it was not known to Paul. In Gal 1:16 (God "was pleased to reveal his Son to me, in order that I might preach him among the gentiles, I did not confer with flesh and blood"), some scholars have suggested that Paul was indicating knowledge of the content of Mt 16:16–17. This is conceivable.[48] But it is highly probable that Paul derived the expression "flesh and blood" not from the Petrine tradition but from common usage, to relate Christ's post-resurrection appearance to him and to draw a contrast between God's revealing power and human weakness. From his explicit references to Peter in Gal 1–2, however, we are justified in concluding that the Galatian Christians knew and had heard about Peter as the most prominent member among Jesus' disciples, and as the "rock" of the first Christian community in Jerusalem.

Whereas Peter recognized the authority of Jerusalem (Acts 10–11), Paul, though also accepting it, was at the same time looking beyond Jerusalem to another important city, Rome. He was anxious to collect money for the poor, the saints in Jerusalem. This activity transcended material help. It was also a sign of Paul's recognition of the importance of Jerusalem, and of the Jewish Christians in the city, for the whole church. Jerusalem, after all, was the place of Christ's crucifixion, resurrection, ascension, the Pentecost and the birth of the first Christian community. In his letter to the Romans, Paul warned the gentile Christians that the Jewish Christians were historically the first to be incorporated in Christ (Rom 11). The gentile Christians, therefore, were "in debt" to them, and "if the gentiles have come to share in their spiritual

---

48 D. J. Chapman, in an article published in the *Revue Bénédictine* 29 (1912), under the title "St Paul and the Revelation to St Peter, Mt 16:17," pp. 137–47, states that his knowledge of Christ is not given by flesh and blood but is revealed by the Father. He "presupposes the words (Mt 16:16–17) to be perfectly familiar to his Galatian converts" (p. 141). Other than in Gal 2:7–8, Paul always uses the name Cephas, and only here does he use the name Peter. Chapman suggests that the reason for this is that Paul has in mind "a Greek document, in which he found Simon Peter's confession, Our Lord's declaration that he was blessed in receiving this revelation" (p. 144). By using the name Peter in Gal 2:7–8, Paul let it be known that "he was fully aware of Peter's position as the Rock" (*A Catholic Commentary on Holy Scripture* [New York, 1953], p. 1115).

blessing, they ought also to be of service to them in material blessing" (Rom 15:25–27). Yet Paul, in the same epistle, expressed a strong desire to reach Rome. And finally, in spite of great odds and dangers, he found himself in the capital of the Empire. Henry Chadwick, analyzing Acts 21–28 and the insurmountable difficulties which Paul had to overcome on the way to Rome, drew the well-founded conclusion that it was Paul, rather than Peter, who contributed more to the creation of Rome as another center equal to Jerusalem.[49]

The figure in the early church who appears more "papal" than either Paul or Peter, it seems to us, is James, the brother of the Lord, who after "much debate" about circumcision at the Council of Jerusalem (ca. 49) finally concludes: διὸ ἐγὼ κρίνω (therefore *I* decide, Acts 15:19). And if the verses of Mt 16:17–19 serve as the basis for a claim to primacy for any particular church, then this church might well be the church at Antioch,[50] where Peter was revered, where Matthew's gospel was written, and where the Petrine passage was transmitted.

Christ's promise to Peter, "I will build my church," was a promise that was fulfilled at the first eucharistic gathering at Jerusalem, with Peter at its head. Jesus had in mind the church as the assembly of God's people, who would commit themselves to him, believe in him, and live their lives according to his will. The Risen Christ also promised that he would be continuously present in the church: "I am with you always, to the close of the age" (Mt 28:20). The primary meaning of ἐκκλησία in the New Testament was, as we have seen, the local church, which embodied the Church Universal, the Catholic Church. In the perspective of the New Testament, no single, local church could possess primacy over other churches. The idea of a universal church, in which each local church is

---

49 See his "The Circle and the Ellipse," in Henry Chadwick and Hans von Campenhausen, *Jerusalem and Rome* (Philadelphia, 1966), pp. 23–36. He ends his discussion with the following observation: "Let it simply be said that the visitor to Rome who passes from the great Church of St Peter's to that of St Paul's-without-the-Walls is struck by the isolation and neglect of the latter. There is perhaps irony here. For if there is one man who more than any other one man may be regarded by the historian as the founder of the papacy, that is surely St Paul" (p. 36.)

50 For G. Downey, Mt 16:18 expresses "the tradition of Antioch concerning the foundation of the Church there. Thus the words in Matthew could form a basis for the claim of the church at Antioch to supremacy over Jerusalem" (*A History of Antioch in Syria from Seleucus to the Arab Conquest,* 1961, p. 283, quoted in R. Brown and John Meier, *Antioch and Rome* [New York: Paulist Press, 1982], p. 67, note 150).

only a part of a larger whole, is not the teaching of the New Testament. Neither is the concept of Peter's trans-apostolic authority.[51]

The words and prophecies of the Gospels, inspired by the Spirit, have life in themselves and are fulfilled in history. The words of Christ have always been applied to the new historical situations in which the church found itself. Under the guidance of the Spirit, their meaning has been revealed. The Spirit, Jesus promised, will teach us "all things, and bring to [our] remembrance all that he had said to us" (Jn 16:13). And yet the Spirit "will not speak on his own authority," but "will take" what belongs to Jesus and "declare it to us" (Jn 16:14–15). The verb ἀναγγέλλειν, translated as "declare" or "re-announce," "re-proclaim," implies that, under the guidance of the Spirit for each generation in subsequent Christian history, the words and deeds of Christ will be interpreted. These verses also suggest that there will be growth or development in our understanding of the words spoken by the Incarnate Lord, as well as an organic, inner correspondence between the "origins" and "develop-ment," between the "seed" and the "tree," between the "foundation" and the "building." The development of the preeminence of Peter in the New Testament (the "seed") to the primacy of Peter ("the tree") at a later stage cannot be understood or interpreted in terms of legitimate growth, but rather in terms of an "evolutionary"[52] process that allowed non-biblical

51 Charles Journet, *Primauté de Pierre dans la perspective protestante et dans la perspective catholique* (Paris, 1953), pp. 74–76. He states repeatedly that in Mt 16:18 Jesus had in mind the universal church, and the power over this church was given to Peter as his personal privilege. Peter received "un privilège transapostolique," which is manifested in his primacy over the universal church.

In contrast, "every true early Christian congregation was just as good a representation of the whole body as the primitive congregation at Jerusalem," writes K. L. Schmidt, *TDNT*, v. III, p. 535. These claims to primacy evolved in the fourth century.

52 C. F. D. Moule, in his book on *The Origin of Christology* (Cambridge, 1977), pp. 2–3, writes about two tendencies in the presentation of Christology. One of these he characterizes as "evolutionary," and the other as "developmental." His view is that "development" or "growth" serves as a better analogy for the origin of Christology than "evolution." Without denying evolution in the field of biology, he doubts its application to historical problems. "Evolution means the genesis of successive new species by mutation and natural selection along the way; "development" by contrast, will mean something more like the growth...of a single specimen from within itself." While in "evolution," "the more complex species generally belong to a later stage...in development, there is nothing to prevent a profoundly perceptive estimate occurring at an early stage." And in the growth or developmental tendency there is no adding of something that is new, "but only drawing out and articulating of what is there." No analogy is perfect, but C. D. F. Moule's simile and its application to the

factors, not inherently present in Mt 16:17–19, to dominate the subsequent understanding of Jesus' promise to Peter.

Let us now see how these verses are interpreted in the early church, before the claims of primacy were raised.

VI

In the writings of some Fathers and Christian theologians of this period, we find a detailed, systematic interpretation of Mt 16:17–19. Surprisingly, however, neither Clement of Rome nor Ignatius of Antioch make any reference to this passage.[53] In the last decade of the first century, Clement, then Bishop of Rome, writes the *Epistle to the Corinthians* in the name of "the Church of God, living in exile in Rome, to the Church of God, exiled in Corinth." He refers to Peter's and Paul's martyrdom in Rome (1 Clem 5:1ff), however, and he mentions Peter before Paul. In this letter, Clement makes no claims to Roman primacy, he neither refers nor appeals to the Petrine text. Ignatius of Antioch, at the very beginning of the second century, on the way to his martyrdom in Rome, writes in his letter to the Romans: "to the church that is in charge of affairs in Roman quarters"; again he refers to Peter and Paul in this order, but he makes no allusions to Peter's primacy. The Bishop of Antioch writes: "I do not give you orders as Peter and Paul did. They were apostles; I am a convict" (Rom 4:3).

It is in Tertullian's *De Praescriptione haereticorum*, ch. 22, that we find

beginnings of Christology can help us in dealing with the interpretation of Mt 16:17–19 and the later claim of primacy. We can conclude that any exclusive claim to primacy (Peter's and Rome's) based upon this Petrine text is an example of the evolutionary tendency, that is, an example of how "alien factors" were added that were not inherent from the beginning.

53 "Omissions of treatment of this passage are very significant. It does not receive the attention from the Fathers that the Roman theory of the primacy of Peter would demand. They composed treatise after treatise with no reference to the passage. For example, there is no citation in the Apostolic Fathers" (Bernard L. Ramm, "The Exegesis of Mt 16:13–20 in the Patristic and Reformation Period," *Foundations* 5 (1962), p. 206).

At the beginning of the third century, we find the first possible use of Mt 16:17–19 to support primacy. The ecclesiastical struggles of this period left their mark upon the exegesis of these Petrine verses. See O. Cullmann, *Peter, op. cit.,* pp. 159, 161, 195; J. Lowe, *op. cit.,* p. 64. Y. Congar, *op. cit.,* p. 144, writes "The first bishop of Rome to appeal to the famous text of Mt 16:18 was Callistus in his edict of indulgence (ca. 220)...for many centuries, it was far from playing such a prominent role in ecclesiology as it is made to do now." But Congar adds that the significance of Mt 16:18 "was only gradually perceived or, at least, expressed."

Mt 16:18–19 explicitly mentioned for the first time in ancient Christian literature.[54] In this passage, the Latin Father addresses the problem of how much the apostles knew and how faithful they were in transmitting the Faith. He is discussing an apparent contradiction in the statements of certain heretics on these questions. Tertullian argues that heretics say, on the one hand, that the apostles did not know all things, and, on the other hand, that the apostles knew all things but did not transmit them to everybody. Those whom Christ ordained to be teachers, whom He kept by him and to whom he explained all things (Mk 4:34), were not ignorant men, Tertullian insists. "Was anything withheld from the knowledge of Peter," adds Tertullian,

> who is called "the rock on which the church should be built" and who also obtained "the keys of the kingdom of heaven," with the power of loosing and binding in heaven on earth? Was anything, again, concealed from John, the Lord's most beloved disciple, who used to lean on his breast, to whom alone the Lord pointed Judas out as the traitor, whom he commended to Mary as a son in his own stead?[55]

Tertullian's references here are important for two reasons. First, in general terms he expresses the view that there was no distinction between the apostles in the degree of their knowledge. Second, after he quotes Mt 16:18–19, he immediately mentions the apostle John, making it quite clear that Peter's knowledge is not greater than John's. He makes no claim for Peter's primacy.

In *De Pudicitia* 21,[56] Tertullian disputes the views of Callistus, the Bishop of Rome, who orders that penance be imposed on those who commit sins of unchastity. Tertullian begins by stating that the apostles have been given the power to forgive sins. But this forgiveness of sins is to be granted "not in the exercise of discipline but of power," which comes from God. Whereas "discipline governs a man, power sets a seal upon him, apart from the fact that power is the Spirit, but the Spirit is God." He then asks the bishop for prophetic evidence

> that I may recognize your divine virtue, and vindicate to yourself the *power* of remitting such sins! If, however, you have had the functions of *discipline* alone allotted you, and (the duty) of presiding not imperially but ministerially; who

54 J. Ludwig, *op. cit.*, p. 11.
55 In *Ante-Nicene Fathers* (ANF), v. IV, p. 253.
56 ANF, v. IV, pp. 98–99.

or how great are you, that *you* should grant indulgence...

Tertullian agrees with the bishop that "the church has the power of forgiving sins," but to him it must be the church of the prophetic Spirit. Finally, he inquires about the basis on which Callistus claims this right to forgive sins. Is it because of Jesus' words to Peter? He quotes Mt 16:18–19 and emphasizes that this promise is conferred personally upon Peter. No bishop has part in Peter's personal prerogatives. "'On *thee*,' He says, 'will I build My Church'; and 'I will give to *thee* the keys,' not to the Church, and 'whatsoever *thou shalt have loosed* or *bound*,' not what *they* shall have loosed or bound."[57]

Tertullian considers Mt 16:18–19 to be a personal promise to Peter, and he makes no distinction here between Πέτρος and πέτρα. The church is built upon Peter personally.[58]

In his controversy with Bishop Stephen (254–257), Cyprian expressed the view that any bishop, whether in Rome or elsewhere, was included in Jesus' message to Peter. Like Tertullian, Cyprian is unwilling to accept the claim of exclusive authority for the Bishop of Rome on the basis of Mt 16:18–19. Unlike Tertullian, however, he understands Jesus' words to Peter as referring to the body, the corporate body of bishops, and not only to Peter personally. While Tertullian, in his fight with Callistus, insists that the church is built upon Peter personally, Cyprian, in his dispute with Stephen, emphasizes that the church is built upon one man.[59] Cyprian is concerned chiefly with the unity of the church, and he bases this unity on Jesus' promise to Peter, to one man. The identity of this man is secondary: Cyprian is defending the principle of unity. Peter is not superior in power to the other apostles, for according to Cyprian all of them are equal.[60]

57　*Ibid.*, p. 99.
58　Also see Tertullian, *On Monogamy* 8: "Peter alone do I find—through (the mention of) his 'mother-in-law'—to have been married. Monogamist I am led to presume him by consideration of the Church, which built upon him, was destined to appoint every grade of her order from monogamists" (ANF, v. IV, p. 65).
59　J. H. Bernard, "The Cyprianic Doctrine of the Ministry," in H. B. Swete, *op. cit.*, p. 246. The author of this essay quotes Hugo Koch's *Cyprian und der Römische Primat* (Texte und Untersuchungen) (Leipzig, 1910): "Dass es Einer war... ist ihm die Hauptsache; dass dieser Eine gerade Petrus war, ist Nebensache" (p. 11). For Cyprian there is only one church, and this one church is built upon one man; although Christ gave equal power to all the apostles, by his authority he ordered the unity of the church by making it begin from a single man.
60　Beside the version summarized in the previous note, there exists another text of *De Unit. Eccl.* 4, which asserts the primacy of Peter and does not mention that the other apostles are equal

In the pre-Nicene period, Origen is the outstanding exegete. He comments on Mt 16:17-19 more than once. Origen interprets Christ's words to Peter as addressed not only to the Apostle Peter, but to every disciple of Christ who confesses him as Peter did. Origen applies the image of the rock to every follower of Christ, who in turn becomes "a Peter." Christ is "the Rock," and all his followers should be called "rocks." Peter is not the only one upon whom the church must be built. Origen bases his interpretation on Eph 2:2, where the apostles and prophets are declared to be the foundation upon which the church is built, Jesus Christ Himself being the corner stone. The following passages give a clear indication of Origen's approach to the problem:

> If we say what Peter said, not by revelation of flesh and blood, but by light from the Father in Heaven having illumined our hearts, we ourselves become as Peter, and are blessed like him, because the very reasons for which he was blessed have extended to us...[61]

Also:

> But if you think the whole church to be built by God upon that one Peter only, what would you say of John the son of thunder or each of the Apostles? Are we to venture to say that the gates of Hades do not prevail against Peter by a special privilege, but prevail against the other Apostles and the perfect? What is said surely belongs to each and all of them, since all are "Peter" and "Rock," and the Church of God has been built on them all, and against none who are such do the gates of Hades prevail. Is it to Peter alone that the Lord gives the keys of the kingdom of Heaven, and will no other of the blessed receive them? But if this privilege is common to all, so also are all the preceding words addressed as it were to Peter. Here "Whatsoever thou shalt bind on earth shall be bound in Heaven" appears said to Peter; but cf. Jn 10:22–23, spoken to all men constituted as Peter was...For all followers of Christ, the spiritual Rock, take their name from the Rock. Being members of Christ, they take from him the name of Christians; but from the Rock, that of Peter.[62]

On the other hand, when Origen is discussing Mt 16:17–19 in a less

with him, either in authority or in honor. Where does this version of *De Unit. Eccl.* 4 originate? It is most probable, according to J. N. Kelly, that this text was also written by Cyprian before he started his dispute with Pope Stephen. In opposing Stephen's claim to primacy, Cyprian clarified his view. Even the so-called "Papal version," writes J. N. Kelly, "does not necessarily conflict with his general teaching, *viz.*, that the Church's unity is to be found in the consensus of all the collective episcopate" (*Early Christian Doctrines* [New York, 1958], pp. 205–6).

61 Origen, *On Matthew*, XII, 9, given in H. Smith, *op. cit.*, v. III, p. 148.
62 *Ibid.*, XII, 10 in H. Smith, v. III, pp. 151–2.

systematic way, he sometimes identifies Peter alone with the rock. In the following passages, for example, where he asserts that Christ promised to build his church on Peter personally, he ignores the distinction between Πέτρος and πέτρα, which he stresses in his main discussions of the passage:

> To that great foundation of the Church, and most solid rock, on which Christ founded the church, is said by the Lord, "O thou of little faith, wherefore didst thou doubt?
>
> Peter, on whom is built the Church of Christ, against which the gates of Hades shall not prevail...
>
> Peter, against whom the gates of Hades prevail not...[63]

These three references should not be regarded as contradictory to the main trend of Origen's exegesis of Mt 16:17–19.

The Fathers of the Antiochian school were particularly influenced by Origen's predominant exegesis. Theodore of Mopsuetsia and Chrysostom link πέτρα with Peter's confession, and the confession with the faith.[64]

We may conclude that the early church Fathers and Christian writers recognized Peter's position of honor and preeminence in the New Testament period. He was the spokesman for the group of the twelve, the leader, the shepherd, and the martyr. Their interpretations of Jesus' promise to Peter—"You are Πέτρος, and on this πέτρα I will build my church"—converge with those of modern exegetes: the rock is Peter. But they also interpreted the rock as Peter's confession. The church is built on Peter, or the church is built upon the rock, which is Peter's confession. We cannot find two distinct groups of exegetes, one of whom states that "the rock is Peter," while the other concludes that "the rock is Peter's confession." In the writings of any given author, one can often find both interpretations simultaneously. Some of these early exegetes in fact go much further than modern theologians and are more "catholic" and more "liberal" than they

---

63 *Ex Hom.* V, 4; *John,* V (fragment 1087 from Eusebius, *H. E.* VI, 25); *First Principles* III, II, 5, in H. Smith, v. III, p. 156.

64 J. Ludwig notices that this exegesis was based upon 1 Cor 10:4 and Rom 10:9 (p. 54). Whereas Origen as well as Eusebius start from 1 Cor 10:4, "the rock was Christ," the Antiochene exegesis of Mt 16:18 rests probably upon Rom 10:9: "If you confess with your lips that Jesus is Lord and believe in your heart that God raised him from the dead, you will be saved." Thus Chrysostom in *Hom.* 54, 3 *On Matthew,* gives us this interpretation: "'Thou art Peter and upon this rock will I build my church,' that is on the faith of his confession."

in asserting that the rock is every disciple of Christ who confesses his Master as Peter did: "You are the Christ, the Son of the Living God."

For these early writers, Peter's leading position does not carry a special status which places him in a class different from all the other disciples of Jesus, nor do they imply that Peter's personal privileges and authority are transmitted to his successors in any particular church.[65] Peter lacked the special authority that a claim of primacy would have given him. He exercised his power in agreement with other leaders in the church.

This early Christian exegesis of the Petrine text appears valuable for three basic reasons. First, it originates in the period before the claim of Peter's primacy is raised, and therefore stays relatively free from the influence of disputes and controversies that plague later centuries. Secondly, both the Greek and Latin writers are in agreement regarding the role and place of Peter in the church. Third, these Fathers live in a world different from that of Peter and are confronted in their own churches with different problems from those that Peter and the apostles had to deal with, and yet they do not introduce "alien factors" into their interpretation of Peter's tradition, but draw their inspiration from the New Testament, and remain faithful to its portrait of the apostle.

---

65 J. N. Kelly, *op. cit.*, p. 408. Let us refer to the testimony of Irenaeus again. He writes: "When the blessed apostles had founded and built up the Church, they handed over the ministry of the episcopate to Linus...Anencletus succeeded him. After him Clement received the lot of the episcopate in the third place *from* the apostles...Evarestus succeeded to this Clement, and Alexander to Evarestus; then Xystut was installed as the sixth *from* the apostles...Eleutherus now in the twelfth place *from* the apostles holds the lot of the episcopate. In this very order and succession the apostolic tradition in the Church and preaching of the truth has come down even to us" (Irenaeus, *Against Heresies*, Book III, 3, in Cyril C. Richardson, pp. 372ff [Emphasis V. K.]).

3

St Peter in Byzantine Theology[1]

John Meyendorff

During the Middle Ages both the Christian West and East produced an abundant literature on St Peter and his succession. They generally drew from the same scriptural and patristic store of texts. However, these texts, first isolated and then artificially regrouped by polemicists, can only recover their real significance if we regard them in a historical perspective and, more especially, within the framework of a consistent and well-balanced ecclesiology. It is this work of "resourcement" and integration which ecumenical thought faces today if it is to reach any concrete result. We will attempt here, in a brief study of the Byzantine texts concerning St Peter, to find out whether we may discern permanent elements of an ecclesiology in the attitude of the Byzantines towards the New Testament texts on Peter, towards the tradition on the specific ministry of the "Coryphaeus," as Peter is often called in Byzantine texts, and finally towards the Roman conception of his succession.

In our work, we shall limit ourselves to the medieval literature subsequent to the schism between the East and the West. At first glance, such a choice of period, when the positions were already clearly defined, might seem to be unfavorable for our purpose. Were not the minds of the writers then engaged in a sterile conflict? Were they still capable of an objective interpretation of Scripture and Tradition? Did they actually contribute to a real solution of the Petrine problem?

We will try to show that, despite the inevitable exaggerations of polemical writings, our Byzantine documents authentically reflect the position of the Orthodox Church in regard to Roman ecclesiology, and have, as such, the value of a testimony very little known, often unpublished, and therefore ignored by a great number of contemporary theolo-

1 In a slightly different form this study appeared in *St Vladimir's Seminary Quarterly*, 4 (1960) No. 2-3, pp. 26-48.

gians. In their attitude toward Peter and the Petrine tradition, the Byzantine writers actually repeat the views of the Greek Fathers, notwithstanding the impact of the contemporary problems upon their arguments. This rigid conservatism explains, to a certain extent, why the development of the Roman primacy in the West remained unnoticed for such a long time in the East. The Eastern Churches had always recognized the particular authority of Rome in ecclesiastical affairs, and at Chalcedon had emphatically acclaimed Pope Leo as a successor of Peter, a fact which did not prevent them from condemning the monothelite Pope Honorius at the Sixth Ecumenical Council in 681. Even in the ninth century they did not realize that their previous acclamations were being interpreted in Rome as formal definitions of the Roman right to a primacy of power (*primatus potestatis*).

The Byzantines unanimously recognized the great authority of the old Rome, but never understood this authority in the sense of an absolute power. The prestige of Rome was not due, in their eyes, only to the "Petrine" character of this church. Indeed, the famous Canon 28 of Chalcedon was for them one of the essential texts for the organization of the Church: "It is for right reasons that the Fathers accorded privileges to old Rome, for this city was the seat of the Emperor and Senate..." The Roman authority was thus the result of both an ecclesiastical consensus and of those historical realities which the Church fully recognized as relevant to her own life, namely, the existence of a Christian Empire. The fact of the Pope's traditional definition as the successor of Peter was by no means denied, but it was not considered as a decisive issue. In the East there were numerous "apostolic sees": was not Jerusalem the "mother of all the Churches"? Could not the Bishop of Antioch also claim the title of successor to Peter? These churches, however, occupied the third and the fourth rank in the hierarchy of "privileged" churches, as established by Canon 6 of Nicaea. But the reason why the Roman Church had been accorded an incontestable precedence over all other apostolic churches was that its Petrine and Pauline "apostolicity" was in fact added to the city's position as the capital city, and only the conjunction of both these elements gave the Bishop of Rome the right to occupy the place of a primate in the Christian world with the consensus of all the churches.[2]

2   Cf. my chapter on "The Roman Primacy in the Canonical Tradition Up To the Council of Chalcedon" in *Orthodoxy and Catholicity* (Sheed and Ward: New York, 1965), pp. 49-78.

As we have said, the Christian East for a long time did not realize that in Rome this primacy of authority and influence was being progressively transformed into a more precise claim. Our task here will be to analyze the reaction of the Byzantines, when they finally understood the real nature of the problem, when they realized that the quarrel over the *Filioque* was not the only factor of opposition between the two halves of the Christian world and, moreover, that the solution to this dogmatic quarrel was impossible without a common ecclesiological criterion.

Such is the broad historical situation in which the problem of Peter was finally perceived by the Christians of the East. In their conception of the nature of primacy in the Church, the idea of "apostolicity" played a relatively unimportant role, since in itself it did not determine the real authority of a church.[3] In the East, the *personal ministry of Peter* and the problem of his *succession* were therefore two distinct questions.

Two categories of documents are of special interest in this field: (1) texts containing an exegesis of the classical scriptural passages concerning Peter, and homilies for the Feast of Ss Peter and Paul (June 29);[4] (2) anti-Latin polemical texts. In this latter category a distinction must be made between writings of the twelfth and thirteenth centuries on one hand, and the more elaborate texts of the great theologians of the fourteenth and fifteenth on the other.

1. Exegetes and preachers

One can safely assert that this category of Byzantine documents was not influenced at all by the schism between East and West. Greek scholars and prelates continued the tradition of the Fathers without the slightest alteration.

It would be impossible for us here to deal extensively with patristic exegeses of the various New Testament *logia* dealing with Peter.[5] We will therefore limit ourselves by referring to Origen, the common teacher of

---

3   Cf. the remarkable chapter on apostolicity before Chalcedon in F. Dvornik, *The Idea of Apostolicity in Byzantium and the Legend of the Apostle Andrew* (Cambridge, MA, 1958), pp. 39–105.

4   Numerous texts have been gathered by M. Jugie, *Theologia dogmatica christanorum oriental-ium*, Vols. I and IV.

5   We may refer the reader to a comprehensive study of the subject by J. Ludwig, *Die Primatwörte Mt. 16, 18, 19 in der altkirchlichen Exegese* (Münster, Westf., 1952).

the Greek fathers in the field of biblical commentary. Origen gives an extensive explanation on Mt 16:18. He rightly interprets the famous words of Christ as a consequence of the confession of Peter on the road of Caesarea Philippi: Simon became the Rock on which the Church is founded because he expressed the true belief in the divinity of Christ. Thus, according to Origen, all those saved by faith in Jesus Christ receive also the keys of the Kingdom: in other words, the successors of Peter are *all* believers. "If we also say," he writes, "Thou art the Christ, the Son of the living God, then we also become Peter [γινόμεθα Πέτρος]...for whoever assimilates to Christ becomes the Rock [πέτρα]. Does Christ give the keys of the Kingdom to Peter alone, whereas other blessed people cannot receive them?"[6]

This same interpretation implicitly prevails in all the patristic texts dealing with Peter: the great Cappadocians, St John Chrysostom, and St Augustine all concur in affirming that the *faith of Simon* made it possible for him to become the Rock on which the Church is founded, and that in a certain sense all those who share the same faith are his successors. This same idea is to be found in later Byzantine writers. "The Lord gives the keys to Peter," says Theophanes Kerameus, a preacher of the twelfth century, "and to all those who resemble him, so that the gates of the Kingdom of heaven remain closed for the heretics, yet are easily accessible to the faithful."[7] In the fourteenth century, Callistus I, Patriarch of Constantinople (1350–3, 1354–63), in a homily for the Sunday of Orthodoxy, gives the same interpretation of the words of Christ to Peter.[8] Other examples could easily be found.

On the other hand, a very clear patristic tradition sees the succession of Peter in the episcopal ministry. The doctrine of St Cyprian of Carthage on the "See of Peter" as being present in every local church, and not only in Rome, is well known.[9] It is also found in the East, among

6   *Hom. in Mat.*, XII, 10, ed. Klostermann, G. C. S. 40 (Leipzig, 1935), pp. 85–9 (PG XIII, 997–1004).

7   *Hom. LV*, PG CXXXII, 965 A.

8   The homily is unpublished; its text is to be found in a manuscript of Patmos (*Patm.* 366, fol. 412v).

9   Cf. in particular A. d'Alès, *La théologie de S. Cyprien* (Paris, 1922), pp. 91–218; P.–Th. Camelot, "Saint Cyprien et la Primauté," in *Istina* 4 (1957) 421-34; M. Bévenot's introduction in Cyprian, *On the Unity of the Catholic Church*, in *Ancient Christian Writers*, 25 (Westminster: Newman, 1957).

people who certainly never read the *De unitate ecclesiae* of Cyprian, but who share its main idea, thus witnessing to it as a part of the catholic tradition of the Church. St Gregory of Nyssa, for example, affirms that Christ "through Peter gave to the bishops the keys of the heavenly honors,"[10] and the author of the *Areopagitica*, when speaking of the "hierarchs" of the Church, refers immediately to the image of St Peter.[11] A careful analysis of ecclesiastical literature both Eastern and Western, of the first millennium, including such documents as lives of saints, would certainly show that this tradition is a persistent one; and indeed it belongs to the essence of early Christian ecclesiology to consider any local bishop to be the teacher of his flock and therefore to fulfil sacramentally, through the apostolic succession, the office of the first true believer, Peter.

In the correspondence and encyclicals of a man like St Athanasius I, Patriarch of Constantinople (1289–93, 1303–10), one can find numerous references to evangelical texts, mainly Jn 21, as pertaining to the episcopal office.[12] His contemporary, Patriarch John XIII (1315–19), in a letter to Emperor Andronicus II, declared that he accepted the patriarchal throne of Byzantium only after an apparition of Christ, addressing him as he once addressed the first apostle: "If thou lovest me, Peter, feed my sheep."[13] All this shows quite clearly that both the ecclesiastical conscience of the Byzantines and their devotion to St Peter express the relation between the pastoral ministry of the first apostle and the episcopal ministry in the Church.

It is therefore comprehensible why, even after the schism between East and West, Orthodox ecclesiastical writers were never ashamed of praising the "coryphaeus" and of recognizing his pre-eminent function

10 *De castigatione*, PG XLVII, 312 C.
11 *De eccl. hier.*, VII, 7; PG III, 561–4.
12 *Letter 61 to emperor Andronicus II*, ed. and tr. by A. M. Maffrey Talbot, *The Correspondence of Athanasius I, Patriarch of Constantinople* (Washington, DC: 1975), pp. 140-1; other letters by Athanasius, yet unpublished and found in the *Vat. gr.* 2219, contain the same idea, cf. *Letter to Bishops, ibid.*, fol. 122v; *Letter to the Metropolitan of Apameia, ibid.*, fol. 128; *Instruction to Bishops, ibid.*, fol. 133v, fol. 154; *Encyclical, ibid.*, fol. 187v; *Letter to the Monks of Athos, ibid.*, fol. 266.
13 Pachymeres, *De Andronico Pal.*, V, 6, ed. Bonn, II, p. 381; for Western sources, representing an identical view of the episcopate as originating in Peter, see Y. Conger, *L'ecclésiologie du haut Moyen-Ages* (Paris: Cerf, 1968), pp. 138-86.

in the very foundation of the Church. They simply did not consider this praise and recognition as relevant in any way to the papal claims, since any bishop, and not only the pope, derives his ministry from the ministry of Peter.

The great Patriarch Photius is the first witness to the amazing stability in Byzantium of the traditional patristic exegesis. "On Peter," he writes "repose the foundations of the faith."[14] "He is the coryphaeus of the Apostles."[15] Even though he betrayed Christ, "he was not deprived of being the chief of the apostolic choir, and has been established as the rock of the Church and is proclaimed by the Truth to be keybearer of the Kingdom of heaven."[16] One can also find expressions in which Photius aligns the foundation of the Church with the confession of Peter. "The Lord," he writes, "has entrusted to Peter the keys of the Kingdom as a reward for his right confession, and on his confession he laid the foundation of the Church."[17] Thus, for Photius, as for the later Byzantine theologians, the polemical argument artificially opposing Peter to his confession did not exist. By confessing his faith in the divinity of the Savior, Peter became the Rock of the Church. The Council of 879–80, which followed the reconciliation between Photius and John VIII, went even so far as to proclaim: "The Lord placed him at the head of all Churches, saying...'Feed my sheep.'"[18]

Was this mere rhetoric, which the Byzantines, to be sure, often abused? The title of "coryphaeus," for example, is often given not only to Peter, but also to other Apostles, especially Paul and John, and does not have a particular meaning. But it is obviously impossible to explain by rhetoric the persistence of an extremely realistic exegesis of the scriptural texts concerning Peter; the "Coryphaeus" was held to be an essential ecclesiastical function.

Peter, Patriarch of Antioch, in a letter to Michael Cerularios, repeats,

14 *Epist. 99 and Niceph.*, PG CII, 909 A.
15 *Epist. I ad Nicolaum,* PG CII, 585 C; cf. *Hom. II on Good Friday,* in C. Mango, *The Homilies of Photius* (Cambridge, Mass., 1958), p. 59.
16 *Hom. I,* in C. Mango, p. 50. Almost the same expressions are used by Photius in a solemn speech delivered to the council of 867, which condemned Pope Nicholas I (*Hom. XVIII,* in C. Mango, p. 312).
17 *Amphil.* 194, PG CI, 933 A.
18 Harduini, *Collectio,* VI, 232 E.

for example, the expressions of Photius when he says that "the great Church of Christ is built on Peter."[19] We find even more explicit texts in Theophylact of Bulgaria, who, at the beginning of the twelfth century, composed commentaries on the Gospels. Explaining Lk 22:32–3, he puts in the mouth of Christ the following words: "Since I make thee the chief [ἔξαρχος] of my disciples (after this thou wilt deny me, thou wilt cry and thou wilt come back to repentance), reaffirm the others; for thus it behooves for thee to act, thou being, after me, the rock and the foundation of the Church." "One must think that this was said," continues Theophylact, "not only about the disciples who lived then, that they might recover in Peter their foundation, but about all the faithful till the end of the ages..." After his denial, Peter "received again, because of his repentance, the primacy over all and the presidency of the universe."[20]

Theophylact also insists on the fact that the words of Christ in Jn 21 are addressed personally to Peter: "The Lord," he says, "entrusts to Peter the presidency over the sheep in the world, to nobody else but him."[21] Elsewhere, he writes: "If James received the throne of Jerusalem, Peter was made the teacher of the universe."[22] In this last text one clearly discerns a conscious theological thought, not mere rhetoric, in the distinction between the functions of James and those of Peter. We shall later see that this distinction is essential in the Byzantine conception of the Church.

The expressions of Photius and Theophylact were taken over by many others, such as Theophanes Kerameus and, in Russia, St Cyril of Turov. Arsenius, a famous patriarch of Constantinople (1255–60, 1261–7), is also no exception to the rule when he writes: "He is indeed blessed, Peter, the Rock [Πέτρος τῆς πέτρας] on which Christ has established the Church."[23]

In the fourteenth century, St Gregory Palamas is to use the same terms. Peter is the Coryphaeus, the "first of the Apostles." In his sermon for the Feast of June 29, Gregory goes even further and compares Peter to Adam. By giving to Simon the name of "Peter" and by building "on

19 PG CXX, 800 B.
20 *In Lucam*, PG CXXIII, 1073 D–1076 A.
21 *In Johannem*, PG CXXIV, 309 A.
22 *Ibid.*, col. 313 A.
23 Quoted by M. Jugie, IV, p. 328.

him" his Church, Christ has made him the "father of the race of the true worshippers of God." Like Adam, Peter was exposed to temptation by the devil, but his fall was not a final one; he repented and was restored by Christ to the dignity of "pastor, the supreme pastor of the whole Church."[24] Palamas is explicit in opposing Peter to the other apostles. "Peter," he writes, "belongs to the choir of the apostles, and yet is distinct from the others, because he bears a higher title."[25] He is, indeed, their personal "coryphaeus" and the "foundation of the Church."[26]

It is not difficult to present an abundance of such quotations. All Byzantine theologians, even after the conflict with Rome, speak of Peter in the same terms as Photius and Theophylact, without any attempt to attenuate the meaning of biblical texts. Their quiet assurance proves once more that they did not think of these texts as being an argument in favor of Roman ecclesiology, which they moreover ignored, and the "logic" of which was totally alien to Eastern Christianity. The following points, however, seemed evident to them:

(1) Peter is the "coryphaeus" of the apostolic choir; he is the first disciple of Christ and speaks always on behalf of all. It is true that other apostles, John, James and Paul, are also called "coryphaei" and "primates," but Peter alone is the "rock of the Church." His primacy has, therefore, not only a personal character, but bears an ecclesiological significance.

(2) The words of Jesus on the road to Caesarea Philippi—"On this rock I will build my Church"—are bound to the confession of Peter. The Church exists in history because man believes in Christ, the Son of God; without this faith, there can be no Church. Peter was the first to confess this faith, and has thus become the "head of theologians," to use an expression of the Office of June 29; he has received the messianic title of the "Rock," a title which in biblical language belongs to the Messiah himself. To the extent, however, that this title depends on a person's faith, one can also lose it. This is what happened to Peter, and he had to undergo tears of repentance before he was reestablished in his dignity.

24 Hom. 28, PG CLI, 356–60.
25 Triads, II, I, 38, ed. Meyendorff (Louvain, 1959), p. 304.
26 Ibid., III, I, 38, p. 630; cf. other references to similar passages of Palamas in my Introduction à l'étude de Grégoire Palamas (Paris, 1959), p. 251, note 126.

(3) The Byzantine authors consider that the words of Christ to Peter (Mt 16:18) possess a final and eternal significance. Peter is a mortal man, but the Church "against which the gates of hell cannot prevail" remains eternally founded on Peter.

2. Polemicists Of The Twelfth To Thirteenth Centuries

As we may easily imagine, the Byzantine anti-Latin texts are far from all being of equal value, and it is not always possible to deduce a consistent ecclesiology from them. A vast number deal with the controversy over the *Filioque*, ignoring altogether the problem of Peter and of his succession. This problem, however, became unavoidable when Byzantine theologians and prelates found themselves face to face with the reformed and tremendously strengthened Papacy of the twelfth century.

Several positions developed on the Byzantine side. The hardest of all used the logic contained in canon 28 of Chalcedon (451), and pushed it to its ultimate conclusions. The organization of the Church follows the "imperial" criterion. "Old Rome" enjoyed primacy because it was the imperial capital. That privilege now belongs to Constantinople. It seems that this logic was predominant at the imperial court. It is expressed quite explicitly by the famous history of Emperor Alexius I Comnenus, composed by his daughter, Anna. The princess considers the idea that the pope presides over the whole *oikoumene* to be an "example of [Latin] arrogance." "The truth is," she writes,

> that when power was transferred from Rome to our country and to our Queen of Cities [i.e. Constantinople], not to mention the senate and the whole administration, the order of seniority between the [patriarchal] thrones was also changed. Henceforth, the emperors bestowed primacy to the throne of Constantinople.[27]

The same view is expressed in 1155 by a metropolitan of Ephesus, George Tornikes in a latter to pope Hadrian IV, written in the name of the emperor, where the author affirms that "the throne of Constantinople is superior to that of Rome."[28] Tornikes is also the author of a *Praise*

27 *Alexiad* I, 13, 3, ed. B. Leib (Paris: Les Belles Lettres, 1937), tome I, 48; tr. E. R. A. Sewter (modified) (Baltimore, MD: Penguin Books, 1969), p. 62.
28 On this document, see G. Hofmann, "Papst und Patriarch unter Kaiser Manuel I. Komnenos," Ἐπετήρις Ἑταιρείας Βυζαντινῶν Σπουδῶν 23 (1953) 74-82 and, particularly, T. Darrouzès, "Les documents byzantins du XIIe siècle sur la primauté romaine," *Revue des études byzantines* 23 (1965) 69-72.

of Anna Comnena, and he was closely associated with the Comnenian dynasty. His views, and those expressed by Anna, are also shared by Nicetas Seides, who in a speech delivered on the occasion of the visit to Byzantium in 1112 of Peter Grossolanus, Archbishop of Milan, discards the "ancient" and purely political primacy of Rome in favor of that of Constantinople, "new Rome," "new Jerusalem" and, indeed, a "city of God."[29]

Another attitude, developed also by Byzantine polemicists during that period, consists in simply denying the primacy of Peter among the apostles and in emphasizing that the powers given to him by Jesus were *also* given to the other apostles (Jn 20:23; Mt 18:18). This position—exegetically rather weak and contradicting the traditional recognition of Peter's personal mission, acknowledged in the patristic tradition—would, of course, be used later (as well as in modern times). It appears in the accounts given in 1136 by Anselm of Havelberg, ambassador of the German emperor Lothar III, after his debates with Greek theologians.[30]

A third, broader vision of the issue, anticipating more developed ecclesiological debates, appears in the Greek account of a *Dialogue* of Emperor Manuel I with Roman cardinals, held in 1166–9.[31] In arguments attributed to Manuel himself, the Greek position consists here of accepting the personal role of Peter among the apostles, but denying his succession in *Rome alone*. Indeed, the mission of all the apostles—and, indeed, of Peter—was a *universal* mission: Peter's role was not limited to any geographic location (as will be the case of bishops and primates of later ages). We know of his activities in Antioch as well as in Jerusalem, but the churches of these places do not pretend to primacy. The primacies of both Rome and Constantinople are of imperial, not divine origin, and they are conditioned by a confession of the true faith: this condition has been broken, in the case of "old Rome," by the addition of the *Filioque* to the Creed.

In the period immediately following the Latin capture of Constantinople (1204), when Rome for the first time decided to appoint bishops to oriental sees, and more particularly to Constantinople, this reaction

29 Analysis of the text, based on *Athen. gr.* 483, by J. Darrouzès, pp. 55–7.
30 PL 188, cols. 1121 C.
31 The *Dialogue* is to be found in *Monac. gr.* 229, and is analyzed by Darrouzès, pp. 74–7.

became stronger. These appointments, made by Innocent III, presented the Byzantines with the challenge of Roman ecclesiology on a practical level. The Greeks could no longer believe that the claims of Ancient Rome were not altering the old canonical procedure of episcopal election, or that Roman centralization was not to be extended beyond the limits of the West.

Historians have more than once described the disastrous effect of the Crusades upon the relations between Christians of East and West. The mutual accusations turned into a real uprising of hatred after the capture of Constantinople by the Westerners in 1204. As is known, Innocent III began by solemnly protesting against the violence of the Crusaders, but finally he decided to profit from the given situation and to act in the same way in which his predecessors had acted in other eastern territories reconquered from the Moslems. He appointed a Latin Patriarch to Constantinople. This action appeared to the whole Christian East not only as a religious sanction of conquest, but as a sort of theological justification of aggression. The election of a Latin Emperor in Byzantium could still be interpreted as being in conformity with the laws of war, but by virtue of what right or custom was the Patriarch of the West appointing his own candidate, the Venetian Thomas Morosini, to the See of St John Chrysostom?

In all the anti-Latin documents of that period we see mention of this so-called "right" of the Pope, a right of which the Eastern Church had no knowledge. All of a sudden the East became more fully aware of an ecclesiological development which had taken place in the West and which it was much too late to stop.

Several short documents, all contemporary to the appointment of Thomas Morosini, reveal to us the shock felt by the Orientals:

(1) Two letters to Innocent III by the legitimate Patriarch of Constantinople, John Camateros (1198–1206), written in 1198-1200;[32]

(2) A treatise, sometimes wrongly attributed to Photius, entitled "Against those who say that Rome is the first See";[33]

---

32 Published with a commentary by A Papadakis and A. M. Talbot, "John X Camaterus Confronts Innocent III: An Unpublished Correspondence," *Byzantinoslavica* XXXIII, 1972, 1, pp. 26-41; cf V. Grumel, *Les régestes des actes du patriarcat de Constantinople*, I, 3 (Paris: Institut français d'études byzantines, 1947), n. 1196; cf. brief excerpts in M. Jugie, IV, pp. 341–2.

33 Published for the first time by Beveridge, *Synodikon sive Pandectae canonum*, II (Oxford,

(3) Two writings of the learned Deacon Nicholas Mesarites, very similar in their contents to the pseudo-Photian treatise: the first in the form of a dialogue with Morosini (a dialogue that actually took place in Constantinople on August 30, 1206);[34] the second pamphlet written when Nicholas already became Archbishop of Ephesus;[35]

(4) The letter of a Patriarch of Constantinople, whose name is unknown, to his colleague in Jerusalem;[36]

(5) An article by an unknown Greek author, "Why has the Latin overcome us?," attacking the appointment of Morosini with particular violence.[37]

These writings contain arguments which are not always mature; for example, some of them (Mesarites, Pseudo-Photius and the author of the anonymous pamphlet) try, for the first time, to oppose the apostolicity of Constantinople, supposedly founded by St Andrew, to that of Rome. F. Dvornik has recently proved the very late origin of the legend on which this conception is based; in any case, the argument was quite irrelevant for the Byzantines, whose really strong and Orthodox point against Rome was a different concept of apostolicity itself.[38]

All the documents present arguments concerning the primacy of Peter among the Twelve and deal with the problem of his succession. The Patriarch's letters insist especially on the first point. The anonymous

1672). This document is now to be found in the critical edition of M. Gordillo, "Photius et primatus romanus," in *Orientalia Christiana Periodica* VI (1940) 5-39; the editor attributes the pamphlet to a writer of the early thirteenth century. This was also the opinion of Russian scholars such as Th. Kurganov, "K izsledovaniiu o patr. Fotii," *Khristianskoe Chtenie* (1895) I, p. 198, and Th. Rosseikin, "Vostochnyi Papism v IXm veke" in *Bogoslovskii Vestnik* (1915) II, p. 421. The arguments recently given by F. Dvornik against the authorship of Photius can be considered as decisive (*The Photian Schism* [Cambridge, 1948], pp. 125–7, and *The Idea of Apostolicity in Byzantium*, pp. 247–53).

34 Ed. A. Heisenberg in *Sitzungsberichte der Bayerischen Akademie der Wissenschaften, Philos., philog. und hist. Klasse*, 1923, 2. Abh.—*Neue Quellen zur Geschichte der lateinischen Kaisertums und der Kirchenunion, II.—Die Unionverhandlungen von 30 Aug. 1206* (München, 1923).

35 Published for the first time by Archim. Arsenii in *Chteniia v obshchestve liubitelei dukhovnago prosveshcheniia* (1891 and 1893); republished by A. Heisenberg in the same *Sitzungsberichte*, 1923, 3. Abh., *Neue Quellen, III—Der Bericht der Nikolaos Mesarites über die politischen und kaiserlichen Ereignisse des Jahres 1214.*

36 Ed. A. Pavlov, *Kriticheskie opyty po istorii drevneishei greko-russkoi polemiki protiv Latinian* (St Petersburg, 1878), pp. 158–68; on the date of the letter (1229–35), see J. Darrouzès, p. 51.

37 Ed. Archim. Arsenii, *Tri stat'i neizvestnago grecheskago pisatelia* (Moscow, 1892) pp. 84–115.

38 Cf. F. Dvornik, *The Idea of Apostolicity*, pp. 289–294.

pamphlet, on the contrary, completely rejects the primacy of Peter, as did the opponents of Anselm of Havelberg. As to Nicholas Mesarites, although he uses as a subsidiary argument the legend of St Andrew, he rightly bases his main argument on the fact that the Orthodox attitude is not a rejection of the primacy, but an interpretation of the succession of Peter which differed from the one given by the Latins.

All the authors, with the exception of the writer of the anonymous pamphlet, call Peter "first disciple," "coryphaeus" and "rock." But John Camateros makes an effort to minimize the scope of these titles by opposing them to other texts of the New Testament; the Church is not founded on Peter alone, but on the "apostles and prophets" (Eph 2:20); if Peter is the "first" and the "coryphaeus," Paul is the "chosen instrument" (Acts 9:15), while James had the first place at the Council of Jerusalem. The unknown Patriarch of Constantinople, in his letter to the Patriarch of Jerusalem, goes even further in his attempt to belittle the role of Peter: "It is impossible," he writes, "for a body to be deprived of its head, and for the Church to be a body without a head," but its Head is Christ. "The head newly introduced by the Latins not only is superfluous, but it brings confusion within the body and is a danger for it."[39] The Romans therefore have the disease from which the Church of Corinth suffered when Paul wrote to it that neither Cephas, nor Paul, nor Apollos, but Christ Himself is the Head.

These arguments against the primacy of Peter, arguments which subsequent Orthodox polemicists will often make their own, are obviously not giving sufficient credit to the personal role of the apostle Peter. Therefore, other parts of patriarchal letters, more ecclesiological in their tenor, are of greater importance for us.

We must first note here the essential distinction made between the function of the apostles and that of episcopal ministry in the Church; the function of Peter, as that of the other apostles, was to be a witness for the whole world, whereas episcopal ministry is limited to a single local church. We have already seen this distinction in the writings of Theophylact of Bulgaria and in the *Dialogue* of Manuel I Comnenus. According to John Camateros, Peter is the "universal teacher." However, he adds, the apostolic council in Jerusalem assigned to Peter the apostolate

39 Ed. Pavlov, pp. 164–5.

to the circumcised, but this limitation was not a geographic one; one should not, therefore, identify the function of Peter with that of the Bishop of Rome, or bind it with Rome alone.[40] The anonymous author of the anti-Latin pamphlet also insists that the apostolic function has never been limited to a specific place.[41] The point is made even clearer in the letter to the Patriarch of Jerusalem:

> Christ is the Pastor and the Master, and he has transferred the pastoral ministry to Peter. Yet we see today that all bishops have this very function; consequently, if Christ has accorded primacy to Peter when granting him the pastoral care, let this primacy be also recognized in the others, since they are pastors, and thus they will be all of them first.[42]

The unknown patriarch interprets the confession of Peter and its consequences in the same way: "Simon has become Peter, the rock on which the church is being maintained, but others have also confessed the Divinity of Christ, and therefore are also rocks. Peter is but the first among them."[43]

Thus the Byzantine theologians explain the New Testament texts concerning Peter within a more general ecclesiological context, and more specifically in terms of a distinction between the episcopal ministry and the apostolic one. The apostles are different from the bishop insofar as the latter's function is to govern a single local church. Yet each local church has one and the same *fullness of grace*; all of them are *the Church in its totality*: the pastoral function is wholly present in every one, and all of them are established on Peter. We shall see how this point is to be developed by later Byzantine theologians; let us stress here that both John Camateros and the unknown writer of the letter to Jerusalem recognize an analogy between the primacy of Peter among the apostles and the primacy of the Bishop of Rome among the bishops.

> Having recognized [writes John Camateros] a certain analogy, similar to the one found in geometry, between the relations of Peter with the other disciples of Christ, on the one hand, and the relations of the church of the Romans with the other patriarchal sees, on the other hand, we must examine whether Peter implied and held in himself the other disciples of Christ and whether the choir of the disciples was subdued to him, obeyed him as a chief and a master, leaving thus to the Roman Church a similar universal primacy. But listening to the

40 Ed. cit., 39
41 Ed. Arsenii, pp. 107–11.
42 Ed. Pavlov, p. 165.
43 *Ibid.*, p. 166.

words of the Gospel, our embarrassment is clearly dissolved.[44]

Here is the conclusion of Camateros:

> We agree to honor Peter as the first disciple of Christ, to honor him more than the others and to venerate him as possessing precedence; we recognize the Church of Rome as the first in rank and honor among equal sister-churches…but we have not been taught to recognize in it the mother of other churches or to venerate it as embracing all other churches.[45]

The unknown patriarch is approximately of the same opinion; he stresses the basic identity existing between all local churches and affirms:

> We recognize Peter as coryphaeus, in conformity with a necessary order. But Peter, not the Pope. For in the past the Pope was the first one among us, when his thought and mind were in agreement with ours. Let the identity of faith be reestablished and then let him receive the primacy.[46]

In other words, the Pope is the successor of Peter only if he remains in the faith of Peter.

In the writings of Nicholas Mesarites and in the text attributed to Photius, we find an identical idea, even more clearly expressed. Mesarites also distinguishes the apostolate from the episcopate. He writes:

> It is true that Peter, the coryphaeus of the disciples, went to Rome; there is in this nothing sensational or extraordinary; in Rome, as in other cities, he was a teacher, not a bishop. For Linus was indeed the first bishop of Rome, elected by the holy and divine apostolic college, and then Sixtus, and, in the third place, Clement, the holy martyr, whom Peter himself has appointed to the pontifical throne. It is not true, therefore, that Peter has ever been bishop of Rome. The Italians have made the universal teacher the bishop of one city.[47]

The following text is even more explicit:

> You try to present Peter as teacher of Rome alone. While the divine Fathers spoke of the promise made to him by the Savior as having a catholic meaning and as referring to all those who believed and believe; you force yourself into a narrow and false interpretation, ascribing it to Rome alone. If this were true, it would be impossible for every church of the faithful, and not only that of Rome, to possess the Savior properly, and for each church to be founded on the Savior properly, and for each church to be founded on the Rock, i.e., on the doctrine of Peter, in conformity with the promise.[48]

44 Ed. cit., p. 37.
45 *Paris gr.* 1302, fol. 272 v.
46 Ed. Pavlov, p. 166.
47 Ed. Heisenberg, *Neue Quellen,* II, p. 22.
48 *Ibid.,* III, p. 34–5.

The doctrine of the succession of Peter in Rome only seems to Mesarites a Judaic narrowing of the redeeming grace. He writes:

If you propose the text *Thou art Peter and on this rock I will build my church*, etc., know that this was not said about the church of Rome. It would be Judaic and miserable to limit the grace and its divinity by lands and countries, denying to it the faculty of acting in an equal way in the whole world. When we speak of the Church One, Catholic and Apostolic, we do not mean, as does the provocative Roman ignorance, the church of Peter or of Rome, or Byzantium or of Andrew, of Alexandria, Antioch or Palestine, we do not mean the churches of Asia, of Europe or of Libya, or the one on the northern side of the Bosphorus, but the Church which is spread in the whole universe.[49]

Leaving aside the polemic bitterness of these texts, it is clear that, faced with Roman ecclesiology, Byzantine theologians defend the ontological identity and the equality in terms of grace of all local churches. To the Roman claim of universalism, based on the institutional center, they oppose the universalism of faith and grace. The grace of God is equally present in each church of Christ, wherever "two or three are gathered in His name," i.e., wherever the Church of God exists in its sacramental and hierarchical fullness.

But then why was the church of Rome vested with primacy among other churches, a primacy "analogous" to the one that Peter had among the Apostles? The Byzantines had a clear answer to this question: this Roman primacy came not from Peter, whose presence had been more effective and better attested in Jerusalem or in Antioch than in Rome, but from the fact that Rome was the capital of the Empire. Here all Byzantine authors are in agreement: the 28th Canon of Chalcedon is for them an axiom. Nicholas Mesarites concedes, it is true, that Roman primacy belongs to an old pre-Constantinian tradition, older than the Christian Empire. It had already manifested itself during the trial of Paul of Samosata: the latter's condemnation by a council in Antioch was first communicated to Rome. According to Mesarites, this primacy was established in order to give the Bishop of Rome a greater authority in defending the interests of the Church before the pagan emperors.[50] But whatever the historical accuracy of this scheme may be, Mesarites' essential idea is that the primacy of Rome, which was established by general

49 Ed. Heisenberg, *Neue Quellen*, II, p. 24; cf. Pseudo-Photius, ed. Gordillo, p. 12.
50 Ed. Heisenberg, *Neue Quellen*, II, pp. 22–3; cf. Pseudo-Photius, ed. Gordillo, pp. 12–13.

consensus, is useful to the Church but must depend on the confession of Orthodox faith.

The first reaction of the ecclesiastical consciousness in the East to the Western doctrine of primacy is therefore not an attempt to deny the primacy of Peter among the apostles, but to interpret it in terms of a concept of the Church which differs from that which had developed in the West.

3. The Theologians Of The Fourteenth And Fifteenth Centuries

Several eminent Byzantine theologians dealt with the problem of Peter in the fourteenth and fifteenth centuries. We will limit ourselves to only four of them: Barlaam the Calabrian, Nilus Cabasilas, Symeon of Thessalonica and Gennadios Scholarios. Their thought is more elaborate and more solid than the first reaction of the Greek theologians of the thirteenth century. The argument based on the legend of St Andrew no longer appears.[51]

The writings of Barlaam the Calabrian, the famous adversary of St Gregory Palamas during the hesychast controversies, had great success in Byzantium; indeed, only his writings against Palamas were destroyed after the Council of 1341. His other writings, particularly his anti-Latin treatises, were preserved and had a certain influence. Barlaam devoted three short treatises to the problem of St Peter.[52] They are in the strict Byzantine tradition. A Greek from southern Italy, Barlaam wanted to present himself as a fervent Orthodox.

His essential argument is that the primacy of Peter is not necessarily bound to the Church of Rome. Like the authors of the thirteenth century, he makes a clear distinction between the apostolate and the episcopal ministry. "No apostle," he writes, "has been appointed bishop in such or such city or land. They had everywhere the same power. As to the bishops whom they ordained to succeed them, they were pastors in various cities and countries."[53] Barlaam then gives an interpretation of the episcopal consecration; if the Latins are right, he thinks, then

> Clement was established by Peter as not only Bishop of Rome, but also as pastor of the whole Church of God, to direct not only bishops appointed by the other

---

51 F. Dvornik, p. 295.
52 One of them is published in PG CLI, 1255–80. The other two are to be found in several manuscripts (*Paris. gr.* 1278, 1218, 2751; *Vatic. gr.* 1106, 1717, 2242; *Marc. gr.* 153, etc.).
53 PG CLI, 1260 CD; cf. 1262 C.

apostles, but those also whom the Coryphaeus himself appointed in other cities. But who has ever called Peter Bishop of Rome and Clement—Coryphaeus? Since Peter, the coryphaeus of the apostles, has appointed many bishops in various cities, which law obliges the Bishop of Rome alone to entitle himself the successor of Peter and to direct the others?[54]

Barlaam defends the ontological identity of the churches, and consequently the equality of their bishops. Concerning the Bishop of Rome, his conclusion is:

The Pope has two privileges: he is Bishop of Rome and he is first among other bishops. He has received the Roman episcopacy from the divine Peter; as to the primacy of honor, he was honored with it much later by the Councils.[55]

As bishop he is equal to the others:

Every orthodox bishop is the vicar of Christ and the successor of the apostles, so that, if all the bishops of the world detach themselves from the true faith and there remains but one guardian of the true dogmas…it is in him that the faith of the divine Peter will be preserved.[56]

Moreover, the apostolic and the episcopal functions not being identical, one cannot consider one single bishop as the successor of one apostle. "Bishops established by Peter are successors not only of Peter, but also of the other apostles; just as the bishops established by other apostles are successors of Peter."[57]

This last point is typical of the East, where no particular significance has ever been attached to the "apostolicity" of certain local churches; were there not scores of episcopal sees pretending, often with full justification, to have been founded by the Apostles? In any case, the hierarchy of patriarchal sees was determined not by their apostolicity, but by the authority which they were holding *de facto*. Rome held the first place only "for the good order of the Church," writes Barlaam.[58] And with the

54 *Ibid.*, 1252 D—1263 C. The difference stressed here between apostles and bishops was already clearly pointed out by the early Fathers. St Irenaeus of Lyons considers Linus as the first bishop of the church founded in Rome by Peter and Paul (*Adv. Haereses,* III, 3, 3, ed. Sagnard [Paris, 1952], p. 104); the same conception is to be found in Eusebius (*Historia ecclesiastica,* III, 2, ed. Bardy [Paris, 1952], p. 98). The tradition according to which Clement, second or third bishop of Rome, was also ordained by Peter goes back to Tertullian (*De praescriptione haereticorum* 32, ed. Kroymann [Vienna, 1941], p. 40). It implies that Peter ordained several consectuive bishops of Rome, but was never himself a bishop.

55 *Paris gr.* 1278, fol. 101.

56 *Ibid.,* fol. 127 v.

57 *Ibid.,* fol. 130.

58 *Ibid.*

authors of the thirteenth century, he acknowledges a certain analogy between the apostolic choir and the episcopal college; in both cases there is one "first" who preserves "good order," granting that the choice of the first bishop belongs to the emperors and the councils.

The works of Nilus Cabasilas (an uncle of the famous Nicholas Cabasilas), who became Archbishop of Thessalonica a few months before his death, are directly dependent on the writings of Barlaam. Usually he simply repeats the expressions of the Calabrian "philosopher" with some additional developments. Thus, he also mentions the two distinct privileges of the Pope: the Roman episcopacy and the universal primacy. Like Barlaam he sees the origin of the primacy in the *Donatio Constantini*, the 28th Canon of Chalcedon, and the legislation of Justinian. But he insists, using some new terms, on the more general problem of Peter's primacy. "Peter," he writes,

> is at the same time apostle and chief [ἔξαρχος] of the apostles, while the Pope is neither an apostle [the apostles having ordained pastors and teachers, but not apostles] nor the Coryphaeus of the apostles. Peter is a teacher of the whole world...while the Pope is but the Bishop of Rome...Peter ordains the Bishop of Rome, but the Pope does not nominate his successor.[59]

To some Latins who say that "the Pope is not the bishop of a city...but simply bishop, being different in this from the others,"[60] Nilus answers that Orthodoxy does not know bishops who would be "simply bishops," the episcopal dignity being directly connected with concrete functions in a local church.

In the light of such a doctrine of the Church, Nilus interprets the words of Christ to Peter. If the Pope is the successor of Peter, inasmuch as he keeps the true faith, it is clear that the words of Christ concerning Peter no longer apply to him when he loses this faith. The true faith, however, can be preserved by other bishops; it is therefore obvious that the Church of Rome is not the only one built on the Rock...The Church of Christ is established on the "theology" of Peter (i.e., on his confession of Christ as God), but all those who have the true faith profess this very theology.[61] Nilus understands Mt 16:18 in the manner of Origen: every true believer is a successor of Peter; but, distinct in this from the Alexan-

59 PG CXLIX, 704 D–705 A.
60 *Ibid.*, 701 B.
61 *Ibid.*, 708 B.

drian theologian, he accepts the full significance of the visible structures of the Church. Origenist exegesis is thus integrated into an organic and sacramental ecclesiology. The guardians of truth and the successors of Peter are for him, as for Barlaam, the heads of the churches, i.e., the bishops. Each member of the Church is, to be sure, firmly rooted on the Rock, but precisely to the extent that he belongs to the ecclesial organism, of which the bishop is head. "There is nothing great in the see of Rome being called the apostolic throne, for each bishop is seated on the throne of Christ and is vested with a dignity higher than that of the angels."[62]

In Symeon of Thessalonica, a theologian and liturgiologist of the fifteenth century, we have another witness to the Byzantine attitude towards Peter and the primacy. For him also the succession of Peter is the succession in the true faith:

> One should not contradict the Latins when they say that the Bishop of Rome is the first. This primacy is not harmful to the Church. Let them only prove his faithfulness to the faith of Peter and to that of the successors of Peter. If it is so, let him enjoy all the privileges of pontiff...Let the Bishop of Rome be successor of the orthodoxy of Sylvester and Agatho, of Leo, Liberius, Martin and Gregory, then we also will call him Apostolic and the first among the other bishops; then we also will obey him, not only as Peter, but as the Savior Himself.[63]

Evidently, these words of Symeon are not a mere rhetorical exaggeration. Every Orthodox bishop, so long as he does not betray his episcopal dignity, is the image of Christ in his Church. The first among the bishops is no exception to the rule: he also is called to manifest the image of Christ in the functions which are entrusted to him, in this particular case, the primacy. It is in this sense that the *Epanagoge* of the ninth century speaks of the Patriarch of Constantinople as the "image of Christ"; this famous text, composed probably by Photius, certainly does not contest the role of other bishops as "images of Christ" in their own churches, but affirms that the particular function of the bishop of the capital city is to manifest this image beyond the limits of his diocese, in the life of the whole Empire.

According to Symeon, the function of primacy, which once belonged to the Bishop of Rome, has not disappeared in the Church. Within

62 *Ibid.*, 724 B.
63 *Dial. contra haereses*, 23, PG CLV, 120 AC.

Christendom, as conceived by the Byzantines, the ancient capital city of the Empire has an intangible place, which it must recover once it returns to Orthodoxy, this being a political necessity as well as a religious one. "By no means did we reject the Pope," writes Symeon;

> it is not with the Pope that we refuse to enter in communion. We are bound to him, as to Christ, and we recognize him as father and shepherd...In Christ, we are in communion and in an indissoluble communion with the Pope, with Peter, with Linus, with Clement...[64]

But the actual Pope, "inasmuch as he is no longer their successor in the faith, is no more the inheritor of their throne."[65] In other words, he is no longer the Pope: "The one whom one calls Pope, will not be Pope as long as he has not the faith of Peter."[66]

In fact Symeon expresses here a doctrine of spiritual gifts which has always been considered as obvious by Orthodox theologians. Each person can always become unworthy of the grace he has received and of the function to which the grace of the Holy Spirit has called him. His unworthiness does not suppress, however, either the gift or the function, which are essential to the life of the Church. The infallibility of the Church is therefore, in the last analysis, the faithfulness of God to His people and can never be identified with a personal infallibility, for God can force no one to be faithful to Him. Each bishop receives a charism for teaching and preserving the truth *in the Church*, in which he was made bishop. If he betrays his function he loses it, but the function remains in the Church and will be assumed by others. This is exactly how Symeon of Thessalonica considers the function of primacy: it exists within the episcopal college, as it existed within the apostolic college, but it implies the unity of faith in the truth.

We find the same ecclesiological motivation expressed by the last of the great Byzantine theologians, and the first patriarch of Constantinople under Turkish dominion, Gennadios Scholarios. "Christ established the Church on Peter," he writes, "as to its being invincible by the gates of hell, i.e., by impiety and heresies, he grants this invincibility to the Church, not to Peter."[67] Peter is "Bishop and Shepherd of the universe," writes Scholarios, quoting John 21,[68]

64 *Ibid.,* 121 AB.
65 *Ibid.,* 120 D.
66 *Ibid.,* 121 C.
67 *On the Procession of the Holy Spirit,* I, ed. Petit-Jugie, II, p. 62.
68 *Letter to Joachim,* IV, pp. 206–7.

but the same cannot be said of any of his successors, the bishops. In agreement with all the other Byzantine authors, Gennadios distinguishes between, on the one hand, the apostolic function, founded on a unique and exceptional Revelation, related to the historical event of Christ's Resurrection, and, on the other hand, the ministry of teaching entrusted within the Church to the bishops. Is not the Church "apostolic" because it was *founded* by the apostles and can add nothing to what has been revealed once and for all to the witnesses of the Resurrection?

> The Apostles were given the wisdom and the grace from the Word which is from above, and the Spirit has spoken through them...but once the foundation of the Church has been accomplished, it was not necessary for this grace to belong to the teachers, as once it belonged to the apostles...It was necessary for the Church not to appear diminished by the absence of that grace, or for the faith to receive a lesser help from the Holy Spirit; but to the teachers, faith was sufficient, and still today, it is sufficient for them.[69]

The fullness of Revelation, given in Christ, is transmitted to us by the Apostles. The Church preserves that Revelation in conformity with its own nature. A sacramental organism, it is solidly established on Peter, who confessed, on the road to Caesarea, the truth of the Incarnation. Wherever there is the fullness of this sacramental organism, there is Christ, there is the Church of God, established on Peter.

In this brief study we do not pretend that we have exhausted the content of the Byzantine writings concerning Peter. The texts that we have analyzed seem sufficient, however, to state the existence of a consensus among the principal Greek theologians of the Middle Ages on some specific points.

First, it is important to note that this consensus does not concern the problem of the personal primacy of Peter among the apostles. Some of the polemicists try to deny it, while the majority simply state that the power of the keys was also given to the other apostles, and that the privilege of Peter is really a primacy and not a power essentially different from that of the other apostles. This negative statement, however, does not sufficiently explain all that the Bible means by the messianic image of the "Petra" or the Rock, an image which Christ applies to Peter alone. The best theologians admit the personal importance of this biblical

69   *On the Procession*, II, p. 63.

image and concentrate mainly on the problem of the *succession* of Peter. Nilus Cabasilas states clearly:

> I do not find it necessary to investigate the authority of the blessed Peter in order to know whether he was the head of the apostles and in which measure the holy apostles had to obey him. There can be here a freedom of opinion. But I affirm that it is not from Peter that the Pope got his primacy over the other bishops. The Pope has indeed two privileges: he is the Bishop of Rome…and he is the first among the bishops. From Peter he has received the Roman episcopacy; as to the primacy, he received it much later from the blessed Fathers and the pious Emperors, for it was just that ecclesiastical affairs be accomplished in order.[70]

For the whole patristic tradition, accepted also by the Byzantines, the succession of Peter depends on the confession of the true faith. The confession is entrusted to each Christian at his baptism, but a particular responsibility belongs, according to the doctrine of St Irenaeus of Lyons, to those who occupy in each local church the very throne of Christ in apostolic succession, i.e., to the bishops. The responsibility belongs *to every one* of them, since each local church has the same fullness of grace. Thus the teaching of the Byzantine theologians agrees perfectly with the ecclesiology of St Cyprian on the "Cathedra Petri": there is no plurality of episcopal sees, there is but one, the chair of Peter, and all the bishops, within the communities of which they are presidents, are seated, each one for his part, on this very chair.

Such is the essential notion of the succession of Peter in the Church in Orthodox ecclesiology. There exists, however, another succession, equally recognized by the Byzantine theologians, but only on the level of the *analogy* existing between the apostolic college and the episcopal college, this second succession being determined by the need for ecclesiastical order (ἐκκλησιαστικὴ εὐταξία). Its limits are determined by the Councils and—in the Byzantine perspective—by the "very pious emperors." There was a First within the apostolic college, and likewise there is a Primate among the bishops. This primacy is in a way a necessary development arising from all the measures taken by the Councils to ensure "ecclesiastical order": the establishment of metropolitan provinces, patriarchates, "autocephalies," etc…

In the Orthodox perspective, Roman ecclesiology appears therefore

70 PG CXLIX, 701 CD,

to have weighed disproportionately the "analogous" succession of the Coryphaeus in the person of a universal primate at the expense of the succession of Peter in the person of the bishop of every local church. This lack of balance appeared little by little in history and may be explained by several historical reasons. The West can only restore this balance by a patient search of the tradition. Yet if the Orthodox are to help in this process, they must themselves initiate a careful study of their own tradition and truly become, in this particular sphere of ecclesiology, the authentic witnesses of the primitive Christian truth.

4

The Church Which Presides In Love

Nicholas Afanassieff

I

Orthodox polemics against the primacy of Rome depend, broadly speaking, on Roman Catholic theology.[1] This is not surprising, since the actual aim of Orthodox theology is to refute arguments put forth in favor of Roman primacy. Now the Catholic doctrine of primacy is founded on their doctrine of the primacy of the Apostle Peter: and therefore Orthodox theologians concentrate their attention on this subject. Exegesis of New Testament texts on the position of Peter results in a discussion between Orthodox and Catholic theologians. Meanwhile, a similar discussion has arisen concerning the oldest Patristic evidence about the Church of Rome. Rome's role in history is also under dispute, and so far no agreement has been reached on the matter. No one denies, today, that she has held a leading position, but we have still to ask what position it was and what was its nature. In other words, we started discussing the primacy of Rome before we raised the question: what is primacy itself? Can primacy—whether of Rome or of any other church—really exist in the Church? This is the really important question, and the answer, whether positive or negative, will help us to work out our own views of the Church of Rome. If we are to solve the problem of primacy within the Church, our starting point must be ecclesiology; i.e., we must ask, does the doctrine of the Church contain the idea of primacy (in its present or any other form), or exclude it altogether? This method can be used to solve problems of exegesis and of history too; it is really the most natural approach, for the problem of primacy is inherent in the doctrine of the Church. We can thus pose the problem of primacy in general, for

1 In this essay I develop ideas which I have already published in an article "La doctrine de la primauté à la lumière de l'ecclésiologie," in *Istina* 4 (1957). Some passages are literally transcribed.

Orthodox and Catholics alike. But we must not think of such a method as involving any renunciation (even provisional) of our confessional allegiances. That sort of thing would only be possible for a bad Orthodox or a bad Catholic. As we study the problem of primacy in general, and especially the primacy of Rome, we must not be ruled by polemical motives: the problem is to be solved to satisfy ourselves and Orthodox theology. The solution of the problem is urgent, since Orthodox theology has not yet built up any systematic doctrine on Church government. And although we have a doctrine concerning Ecumenical Councils as organs of government in the Church, we shall see presently that our doctrine is not enough to refute the Catholic doctrine of primacy.

II

1. Approaching our solution of the problem of primacy by a method which we might call "ecclesiological," we are at once faced with a great difficulty: several systems of ecclesiology have grown up in the course of history. And the Church, although itself the subject of all these systems, is understood by each of them in a different way. Therefore, inevitably, the problem of primacy must be stated and resolved differently in each system—and then the several systems will often turn out to be just different facets of the same ecclesiological theory.

The systems can all be reduced to two fundamental types: universal ecclesiology and eucharistic ecclesiology. The universal sort is now predominant, especially in Catholic doctrine. The Orthodox Church has not clearly defined her attitudes, but our "school" teaching follows Catholic doctrine and accepts universal ecclesiology as an axiom.

According to universal ecclesiology, the Church is a single organic whole, including in itself all church units of any kind, especially those headed by bishops. This organic whole is the Body of Christ or, to return to Catholic theological terms, the Mystical Body of Christ. Such a concept of the Church has become a habit of thought and we never question it; we are more inclined to use it to furnish premises on which to build all theological discussions about the Church. But as for finding out the relationship between the different church units, particularly the diocesan church and the universal Church—*that* question is still not quite clarified. Usually the church units are regarded as parts of the universal Church: less often people see in each church a *pars pro toto*, or again a detached fragment, *ein Splitter.*[2] In the Russian ecclesiological system of our time, the episcopal church (the diocese) forms one part of the autocephalous Russian Church. The Moscow Council of 1917–18 decided that "the diocese is defined as one part of the Russian Orthodox Church, when governed by a bishop according to canon law."

This definition of the diocese is incontestable proof that the members of the Council were taking their stand on universal ideology, and that they went further in this respect than the Church of Byzantium. According to the prevalent Byzantine point of view, patriarchates were made up of a number of metropolitan units, and a metropolis was made up of diocesan churches. As history went on, the metropolis tended to decay and the power of the patriarchs increased, but the diocesan churches were always regarded as fundamental units which made up a patriarchate. Hence at Byzantium it was unthinkable for any one to define the diocese (officially at least) as they did at Moscow. When Byzantium was already in decline, a theory arose of the κηδεμονία πάντων. The whole of the Orthodox Church was to be one organic unit, with the Patriarch of Constantinople at its head. The bishops, especially metropolitan bishops, were to be no more than his delegates. The proposed doctrine was out of step with the march of history and did not influence church order.

2. The basic principles of the "world-wide" theory of the Church were formulated by Cyprian of Carthage. A Roman by education and habit, Cyprian may have thought that the mere empirical unity of a number of local churches could not be properly guaranteed. Church membership had increased so much, compared with what it was in the time of the apostles, that Tertullian could now tell the Roman world (with a touch of exaggeration, of course): "The Christian newcomers have filled the place up: cities, islands, fortresses, boroughs, camp and Senate-house, palace and forum—leaving the pagans nothing but their temples." The "Ecumenical Church" (i.e., a number of local churches

2 See O. Linten, *Das Problem der Urkirche in der neuer Forschung* (Uppsala, 1932); F. M. Braun, *Aspects nouveaux du problème de l'Eglise* (Fribourg, 1942) (translation from the German *Neues Licht auf die Kirche,* 1946).

united by concord and love), though a generally accepted idea in Cyprian's time, must have been too vague for him, with his Roman training in precise legal formulae. He saw that the concord of local churches was often broken in daily fact; concord turned into discord, and love into enmity. Human vanity and ambition were leading heretics and schismatics far from the church, tearing and weakening it in the process. On the other hand, there seemed another possibility in Cyprian's eyes, a different unity which seemed next to perfect. Cyprian did not have to live through the awful drama forced on Jerome and his contemporaries, who really came to believe that the fall of Rome would mean the fall of the whole civilized world. Rome was still there, solidly established: the portents foreboding crisis could not yet be observed by the men of Cyprian's time. The entire οἰκουμένη—the inhabited earth, the then universe—was transformed and made one single entity by the strength of the Roman imperial idea: they were one Roman Empire. The government of Rome had gradually become a world-wide system: the whole world looked to it for its fate. Different provinces might be able to live their own lives and even enjoy some autonomy, but they could not break up the organic singleness of the Empire; imperially considered, they were secondary elements. The Roman Empire formed the σῶμα, and the Emperor was its soul. The concept of the Empire was Cyprian's inspiration, though he may not have known it, and the foundation for his doctrine of Church unity. We moderns can no longer imagine the enormous fascination of the Imperial Idea, as leading church figures felt it then. Cyprian turned over a new page of history by his doctrine of church unity, but he also stood on the border-line between two periods: beside having a natural attachment to his own age and to all the Church's past, he was fired by new thoughts when it came to his doctrine of the Church.

To Cyprian, as to Ignatius and Tertullian, the Church is one because Christ is one: *Deus unus est et Christus unus, et una ecclesia.*[3] Here was truth unquestionable, and neither Cyprian nor his contemporaries doubted it. Cyprian was a bishop first and foremost, trying to apply the doctrine of church unity to the changes and chances of the day. He was less interested in the theoretical aspects or intrinsic value of doctrine. The

3   *Epist.* XLIII, V, 2; cf. Tertullian, *De Virg.*, 2.

Church in its empirical *esse*, the one and only Church, appeared to exist in the form of a multitude of churches. How could the unity of the Church be preserved despite the multiplicity of churches? Cyprian answered the question by applying St Paul's doctrine to these many churches, i.e., the doctrine of the organic nature of the Church's body. Just as we can distinguish members in the Church, the Body of Christ, so the one and only Church, physically speaking, is made up of different local churches, which are her limbs or members: *ecclesia per totum mundum in multa membra divisa.*[4] The Church is naturally ecumenical, since she spreads throughout the world and embraces all the churches— those flourishing at a given time, and churches of the past and future as well. Fullness and unity are the possessions of this Church scattered *per totum mundum*, not of isolated local churches which, being merely *members* of the Church, can only possess part of that fullness. Any local church is not the "Catholic" Church, St Ignatius of Antioch taught: the local churches taken all together form the universal, ecumenical Church, i.e., the Catholic Church. So the sense of the term "Catholic Church" has changed; or, more accurately, the concept of "Church" has changed, while the concept καθολικός is the same as it was for Ignatius. For this reason "Catholic Church," empirically speaking, means the same thing to Cyprian as "Ecumenical Church"—the Church on earth at a given time. All the local churches together are the one and only Body of Christ, but the empirical Church is to some extent the sum of its separate parts. Hence Cyprian could speak of *conexa et ubique coniuncta unitas catholicae ecclesiae ;*[5] the unity of the Catholic Church, tied together and cohering. The different parts or members of this Church are joined (*conexa*) like the branches of a single tree or put together (*conjuncta*) like the simple words in a compound word. Cyprian also describes all the local churches taken together as the composite unity of the Church's body, *compago corporis ecclesiastici*:[6] a union, or whole, comparable to the union of a human soul and body. We might say that the empirical whole, the *compositum* (*compago*), is the body of the Catholic Church.

The universal Church, therefore, having catholicity as one of its

4 *Epist.* LV, XXIV, 2; cf. *Epist.* XXXVI, IV, 1. "*Omnes enim nos decet pro corpore totius ecclesiae cuius per varias quasque provincias membra digesta sunt, excubare.*"
5 *Epist.* LV, XXIV, 2.
6 *Epist.* LV, XXIV, 3.

attributes, is a single being divided into various parts. While remaining one, this being manifests itself in everyday life as an assembly of local churches, but its unity is maintained. Cyprian was concerned to know how and why: his quest for an answer led him to construct his theory of the universal Church. Cyprian found this answer in a doctrine of episcopal unity built on almost the same lines as the doctrine of Church unity. The Church is one because there is one God, one Christ, one faith. *Episcopatus unus est*,[7] because "the throne of Peter is one,"[8] "in which God has established and shown the source of all unity."[9] "There is one God alone, one Christ, one Church, one Throne of Peter, whom the word of the Lord had made his foundation-stone."[10] This Throne of Peter is held by the whole episcopate, so that every bishop is Peter's successor, but only insofar as he is part of the episcopate. Cyprian uses the legal term *in solidum* when he affirms that *Episcopatus unus est, cuius a singulis in solidum pars tenetur*:[11] that is, every member of the one episcopate possesses the chair of Peter in common with his fellows. In actual life the episcopate is made manifest in a multiplicity of bishops. "Just as the one Church of Christ is divided into many members throughout the world, so the one episcopate is expanded into a multiplicity of many bishops united in concord."[12] Perhaps it would be more exact to restate Cyprian's thought as follows: the division of the Catholic Church into local churches is the practical result of diffusing the one episcopate into a visible multiplicity of bishops. Every bishop presides separately over his own local church, but all bishops have possession of Peter's throne together and so form a "multiplicity in concord" (*concors numerositas*). This sum of the local churches form a *corpus* in which each church is joined to all the rest by very strong ties: in the same way the bishops too form a *corpus* in which each bishop is joined to all the rest by

7   *De Unit.* V.
8   *Epist.* XLIII, V, 2.
9   *Epist.* XLIII, VII, 1.
10 *Epist.* XLIII, V.
11 *De Unit.* V.
12 *Epist.* LV, XXIV, 2: "*et cum sit a Christo una ecclesia per totum mundum in multa membra divisa, item episcopatus unus episcoporum multorum concordi numerositate diffusus...*" My own text gives a literal translation. I quote the more polished version of Canon Bayard: "Seeing therefore that by Christ's institution there is one Church only in all the world, spread abroad in many members, and one episcopate only, represented by a multiplicity of bishops one in fellowship together..." (St Cyprian, *Correspondence,* II [Paris, 1925], p. 147).

the harmony prevailing throughout the entire episcopate. Full and perfect concord, a quasi-musical harmony, is, in historical fact, to bind the bishops in one.[13] In an ideal world, the unity of the episcopate derives from the unity of the Church: in actual fact the unity of the episcopate preserves the unity of the local churches, since concord among the bishops ties, or rather welds, all these churches into mutual fellowship. Union of the bishops in concord produces a single entirety: and the "symphonic multiplicity" of the bishops in turn makes the local churches into a single entirety. No wonder Cyprian attached such exceptional importance to concord! In his eyes there was no possibility of discord between bishops, because of their common possession of Peter's throne: in effect, this common possession really implies the summary banishment of a member no longer in accord with the rest, and therefore no longer qualified for his share in the episcopate. In this manner, concord and unity are for ever unbroken.

The Church of Cyprian's doctrine might well be compared to a truncated cone: the larger inferior base of the cone would be the numerous but united local churches, and the small top platform the "multiplicity united in concord" of the bishops. Every point on the large base where there is a local church, a member of the universal Church, has its corresponding point on the smaller and higher plane in the bishop, a member of the episcopate: put the other way round, each part of the episcopate (bishop) is responsible for one part of the universal Church. The unity of the top and bottom planes is maintained by their ties with one another. Each may become larger or smaller, but always related to the other, so that if the top level increases in size the bottom does too, and *vice versa.* If any point or part of either level became detached, there would be a corresponding fraction in the other: the cone would then be reduced in size, though still a cone, but the broken-off section would then be outside the cone.

Cyprian defines the relation between bishop and church in a famous phrase: "It must be known that the bishop is in the Church and the Church in the bishop: any person who is not with the bishop is not in the Church."[14]

---

13 *Epist.* LIX, XIV, 2: *"concordia cohaerens."*
14 *Epist.* LXVI, VIII, 3: *"Scire debes episcopum in ecclesia esse et ecclesiam in episcopo et si qui cum episcopo non sit in ecclesia non esse."*

A bishop cannot exist without a Church, but also a Church cannot exist cut off from its bishop: the bottom side of the cone cannot be detached from its top. The top cannot exist by itself, for then the throne of Peter would have no Church in which to be. No more can the base exist without its top, for then the Church would be living without Peter's throne, which Christ founded to hold its unique position there. The Universal Church is the entire truncated cone, and not just one of its surfaces.

There is ample logic in Cyprian's doctrine, but logic by itself is no proof of the truth. So arguments in favor of Cyprian's system must not be founded only on its logical character—its more-or-less logical character, assuming rather that Cyprian's system has been left logically incomplete. In this, however, Cyprian shows the greatest of his doctrinal virtues. An intimate awareness of the Church was the root of his own life; he could not abandon the traditional doctrine of the Church to round off this system. He did not draw from that system the conclusions it implied, any more than he did in general for the other doctrines he put forward. Cyprian's genius comes out in his active Church life more than it does in his theological thought. To posterity he has left an ideal picture of "the Bishop" which shines so brightly and clearly that our minds really see it; he has left us a literary heritage broken by frequent self-contradiction, which has been a matter for controversy from then until the present day. The truncated cone is incomplete in itself. Cyprian had all the *data* for making his cone perfect: according to his doctrine there should have really been one single bishop at the head of the Universal Church. He was unwilling to place the Bishop of Rome outside the *concors numerositas* of bishops, and yet the place given by him to the Roman Church did raise it above the "harmonious multitude." The ideal "Peter's throne" occupied by the whole episcopate became confused in Cyprian's mind with the actual throne occupied by the Bishop of Rome. According to Cyprian, every bishop occupies Peter's throne (the Bishop of Rome among others), but the See of Peter is Peter's throne *par excellence*. The Bishop of Rome is the direct heir of Peter, whereas the others are heirs only indirectly, and sometimes only by the mediation of Rome. Hence Cyprian's insistence that the Church of Rome is the root and matrix of the Catholic Church.[15]

15 *Epist.* XLVIII, III, 1: *"Ecclesiae catholicae matricem et radicem."*

The subject is treated in so many of Cyprian's passages that there is no doubt: to him, the See of Rome was *ecclesia principalis unde unitas sacerdotalis exorta est.*[16] But he does not proceed to draw any conclusions from his doctrine about the See of Rome. Being so keenly aware of the Church's actual life, Cyprian could not deny that the See of Rome held a preponderant position: but he was intuitively in step with trends in the whole Church which did not allow him to make the Bishop of Rome head of the episcopate. The Bishop of Rome undertook to relieve him, and drew the necessary conclusions himself. Logically it was inevitable. If the Universal Church, as Cyprian saw it, can be compared to a truncated cone, we must admit that the upper plane is in fact above the multitude of local churches. It is at the head of the multitude, so to speak, because the power in the Church belongs to it and, through it, also belongs to each bishop in his church. The world-wide unity of the Church cannot be built upon the model of the Roman imperial unity unless we bring in the fundamental principle which held the Empire together—lawful right. Cyprian certainly brought a legal element into his consideration of power inside the Church, but he refused to stretch it to cover the relationship of bishops with one another. The *concors numerositas* of bishops constitutes the power within the Church, but within its own membership it disallows the power mutually united on a foundation of concord. No wonder Cyprian's system turned out to be a historical failure! In his declining years Cyprian was to see his system crash before his own eyes. He saw that the *concors numerositas* was only an ideal; in real life there is certainly *numerositas*, but not concord, since a *corcors numerositas* cannot work without a head.

3. I have dwelt at length on the interpretation of Cyprian's theory of the Church for two reasons. As I said above, he was the first to formulate the principle of a universal theory of the Church. More important still, Cyprian did not succeed in constructing his system without some idea of primacy, and this shows that if a universal theory of the Church is adhered to, the doctrine of primacy will somehow be a necessary concomitant. A single body must be crowned by a single head, showing in his own person the unity of the whole system. If we take the universal theory of the Church, we cannot refute the doctrine of universal primacy

16 *Epist.* LIX, XVI, 1.

just by saying that the Church has Christ as Head; that is an indisputable truth, and supporters of primacy do not themselves oppose it. The real question is: If the Church has an invisible Head (Christ), can she, or can she not, also have a visible head? If not, then why can a local church have a single head in the person of its bishop? In other words, why can one part of the Universal Church have a single head, while the entire Universal Church is deprived of one? This question should be relevant in discussing autocephalous Orthodox churches and their problems. If there is no primacy in the Universal Church, why do we allow a partial primacy within the boundaries of an autocephalous church? The head of an autocephalous church makes manifest its unity: but how can the unity of the whole Orthodox Church be given empirical expression in the absence of a universal primacy? Orthodox theology makes it a point of principle that the Universal Church should be directed by Ecumenical Councils. Obviously, Orthodox theology has made Cyprian's doctrine her own (in part at least): for he constructed the only theological foundations upon which a theory of councils in the Church could rest. Even so, his doctrine on councils remains as incomplete as the rest of his system. The *concors numerositas* of the bishops is naturally manifested in the councils, where their concord should find means of expression. But the concord is only an ideal one, if the element of jurisdiction is never present in the relations between bishops. Also, the decisions of the council have no real weight if they are not founded on legal right. How can they ever be put in force, and by whom? Cyprian certainly thought that these decisions were put into practice by the bishops, who were members of the council and invested with power inside the local churches. The thing was possible, provided the power of the bishops had rested upon a juridical basis, but in Cyprian's time no such basis yet existed—or only in his mind, not in real life. What is even more important, if councils are to manifest the unity of the episcopate, they presuppose primacy within the episcopal body. Without it, who would convoke the councils? Cyprian never asked himself that question, just as he never remarked on his own actual possession of the primacy in North Africa, though that primacy was much more worthy of the name than the primacy of the Bishop of Rome over Italian affairs. We should note that councils have not remained the same in the course of centuries: they have undergone great changes. Cyprian started a new form of councils, episcopal conferences; but his own mental picture saw them in the shape of a diocesan synod enriched by the presence of other bishops. For this reason he was able to avoid asking a whole series of further questions, such as how the council was to be convoked and in what way its decisions could be practically applied. Cyprian's doctrine of councils was to be completed by others, and its final shape was something he could never have foreseen: the Church of the Empire worked it out, and the council of bishops became the council of the Empire.

The conciliar idea cannot be set up against primacy: not only does a council not exclude primacy, it actually presupposes it. The councils cannot be gathered together automatically; they must be convoked by the head of the diocese.[17] If there had been no single heads in the autocephalous churches, councils could never have existed; otherwise, anarchy would have reigned, with every bishop thinking he had a right to convoke councils. The Ecumenical Councils were not "at the head" of the Church; even in the period of their greatest importance, they did not regard themselves as organs for directing the Church. An ecumenical council was certainly the highest institution in the Church: it tackled dogmatic problems and determined the basic principles of ecclesiastical order and discipline. Still, if they were really to stand at the head of the Church, the ecumenical councils should have been permanent, and not convoked in such a random way. It is now commonly accepted that the right of convoking councils belongs to the emperor. However considerable in numbers, a council was still not considered to be a real ecumenical council unless the Emperor had convoked it. The letters of Pope Leo the Great and the emperors Theodosius and Marcian are of great interest here: the Pope, in spite of not recognizing the Council of Ephesus in 449, dared not convoke an ecumenical council himself; all he did was to make insistent statements to the emperors that such a convocation was necessary. The Emperor Marcian, after his accession, decided to convoke a council; and Pope Leo had to bow to the Emperor's opinion, although he thought a convocation would be ill-timed just then, when there had been so many changes both in Church and State. No matter how we define the place of the Roman or Byzantine emperor in the Church, we

17 See Canon 19 of the Council of Antioch.

must accept the fact that he really was, in some ways, the head of the Church-in-the-Empire. Of course it was not primacy that the Emperor held claim to; primacy is an exclusive Church affair and can only belong to a bishop. But if the ecumenical church (the church dwelling inside the boundaries of the Empire) had not had the emperor at its head, ecumenical councils would not have taken place in fact or in principle. When the force of events had turned the ecumenical council into a purely Church institution, councils could not be convoked except where primacy in fact already existed: thus in the West, councils continued to exist even after the separation of the churches, because the primacy of the Bishop of Rome was firmly established there. In the East there were no more ecumenical councils. All attempts to convoke a pan-Orthodox council in our own age have not succeeded, and it is rather unlikely that such a council could ever be convoked. This is due to the absence of a primacy capable of commanding ,recognition by all the Orthodox churches. There is no pan-Orthodox Head of the Church, consequently any convocation of a council is a practical impossibility. Supposing that the leaders of the autocephalous churches should all agree to allow a patriarch to convoke an ecumenical council, their action would imply that this patriarch was recognized as primate of the Orthodox Church. I shall put off any attempt to decide whether the Patriarch of Constantinople has the right to convoke a council, and confine myself to a single remark: ever since the ninth century the *de facto* position of the Patriarch of Constantinople has favored his claim to this right, and yet the Patriarch is well known never to have convoked an ecumenical council: he has never even explored the possibilities of planning such a convocation. One thing is clear: if the autocephalous churches had recognized the right of the Patriarch of Constantinople to convoke, they would simultaneously have recognized his primacy in the Orthodox Church.

I must once more point out the error of basing arguments against primacy on the conciliar principle. Orthodox theologians are nonetheless right in emphasizing the principle, because it defines both the nature and the limitations of primacy. The conciliar principle serves to limit the power of the primate-bishop, but we must not think that this is a hard and fast limitation in legal terms. There is another way to describe it. The bishop possessing primacy acts with the agreement of the whole body of bishops: this agreement is made manifest in the council in which the primate bishop participates as its president. In Orthodox theology, the patriarch is conceived of as being *primus inter pares* among the bishops. This formula, though generally allowed, is misleading, and it would be difficult to find justification for it anywhere in the history of the Orthodox Church. It is indeed doubtful that the bishops ever thought themselves the equals of the patriarch in every respect, or that he thought himself their equal. Equality is really a difficult claim, when the patriarch possesses rights of which the other bishops are deprived. A fairer statement (to use language borrowed from Cyprian of Carthage) would be: the patriarch as member of the episcopate of the autocephalous church is not above it, but as its leader he is first in the episcopal body.

4. The decline of the conciliar principle led to another type of universal doctrine of the Church: we might call it "pontifical." In the West, traces of this doctrine can be found quite early. It becomes dominant after the Council of Trent, which confirmed the idea that the Bishop of Rome had sovereignty over the council. The Pope is superior to the council: the conciliar principle is therefore wiped out. The councils, if they occur, are no longer councils in the true sense of the word, and become advisory agencies supporting the Bishop of Rome. The accord of the episcopate remains a matter of importance, but the Pope is not juridically bound by the decisions of his council. The Pope, placed above the council, becomes superior to all the other bishops and turns into a "super-bishop." But the doctrine concerning bishops is founded on divine law (those are the terms used in Catholic canon law) and still retains its full validity. In the present day, we are witnessing various attempts to introduce important changes into the universal doctrine of the Church, and these changes would affect one particular sphere—the doctrine of episcopacy. According to Catholic and Orthodox theology, a bishop holds first place in the ecclesiastical hierarchy. To him belongs the highest sacerdotal degree; the second degree belongs to the priesthood. Whatever the powers of the bishop may be in matters of government, in matters of liturgy the sum of his powers is always constant. On this principle the powers of patriarchs, autocephalous church leaders, and even popes are identical, liturgically speaking, with the powers of all other bishops. Theologians of today always agree that the difference

between a bishop and a priest, in the sphere of liturgy, has one essential or even exclusive characteristic: that is, the priest cannot celebrate the Sacrament of Ordination. Consequently, certain well-defined powers in matters of liturgy are attached to both classes, and these powers must remain unchanged.

Some thirty years ago, documents were found proving that in the fifteenth century the popes used to allow the abbots of certain abbeys a right to ordain not only minor clerics, but priests as well, in order to serve the needs of their abbeys. This discovery caused a sensation in Catholic circles and led to some embarrassment. Clearly the discovery was to be extremely important to Catholic dogma: it saps the very foundations of the doctrine which declares that bishops alone are entitled to conduct the ordinations of priests. We now know that the superiors of certain abbeys (in other words, priests and not bishops) were able to ordain other priests. The deduction follows: the reason why priests have no right to ordain other priests is not a dogmatic reason but more a question of discipline. The *sacerdotium* with which the priests were invested at their ordination did confer on them power to celebrate the Sacrament of Ordination, but the ecclesiastical authorities debarred them from making use of this spiritual capacity, and the bar was a disciplinary one. If we acknowledge that priests have at least theoretical right to conduct ordinations, should we not admit that there is no difference between priests and bishops where liturgy is concerned, i.e., we have only one degree of *sacerdotium* before us, not two? In that case, the bishop will be nothing but a priest who has been given wider powers in the sphere of jurisdiction.

What are the possible results of such a doctrine of priests and bishops? A contemporary Catholic theologian writes:

Christians must be more than ever one, they must more than ever take their stand in face of all the problems of life, there must be more unanimity in action than ever: one man alone can direct, one alone can teach, one alone command—Peter and his successors. We must not be surprised at this: the former responsibility of the bishop in his diocese is gradually changing hands; and today the Pope will take it over as his own mission; it would not be good, either for the Church or the world, if different, sometimes even conflicting, ideas were adopted by each different diocese. If the Church wants to remain one in a world in process of unification, then the Papacy must speak often and guide all. For this reason, the twentieth century is a new dawn in the Church, the dawn of a new age, a Pontifical age, as it is also the dawn of a comprehensive world and an international society: just as separate states will disappear, so bishops will lose their sovereignty, and leave to Peter and his successors the general guidance of the whole Catholic movement and their whole apostolic charge.[18]

We are indeed witnessing the birth of a new age in the Catholic Church—the birth of a "universo-pontifical" ecclesiology. This new type of ecclesiology is the normal development of universal ecclesiology to its absolute form: on the other hand, it can be interpreted as a sort of return to traditional ecclesiology, though the tradition has undergone much change and some distortion. The great primitive ecclesiastical maxim was that in the Church there must be one bishop only. Ignatius of Antioch gave special importance to the formula, "One God, one Christ, one faith, one altar, and one bishop." We shall see presently that Ignatius, in writing these words, had in mind the local church, and that his ecclesiological context was not at all the same as the Universal ecclesiology. If the Universal Church is a sole body and if we accept Ignatius' statement, we cannot avoid coming to the conclusion that in the Universal Church there must be one single bishop, and that according to Catholic doctrine he can be no other than the Bishop of Rome. In the capacity of being bishop of the entire Universal Church, he takes the place of all the other bishops. In consequence, the others become mere administrative instruments, used by the Pope for governing the innumerable parishes led by presbyters.

It is still too soon to tell if Rome is likely to sponsor this new ecclesiology, which is sturdily opposed in Catholic theological circles.[19] What matters to me is simply the fact that this trend exists in ecclesiological theory. I cannot discuss these new trends here; they would take me too far from the main point. This type of ecclesiology must start with the doctrine of bishops, which is quite a different subject. Furthermore, the ecclesiology of a Universal Pontiff no longer contains any real doctrine of primacy, whatever meaning we may attach to the word; for primacy

18 J. Beyer, S.J., "Le souverain Pontife, centre vital et unité de l'Eglise," *Textes des conférences données au congrès eucharistique des dirigeants de la Croisade eucharistique en août 1955 à Nivelles,* Monthly bulletin of the Directors of the C.E., 24/2 (1955) 38. I quote after B. Luykx, O. Praem, "De l'évêque," in *Questions Liturgiques et paroissiales* (1956) 4–5.

19 See Dom O. Rousseau, "La vraie valeur de l'épiscopat dans l'Eglise," and Dom B. Botte "Presbyterium" and "Ordo episcoporum," in *Irénikon* XXIX/1 (1956).

presupposes a multiplicity of bishops among whose number one holds the primacy.

5. We can now form our first conclusions. Universal ecclesiology (which says that the entire Church on earth is a unique living body) contains in itself the doctrine of a single man as head of the Church. It must be admitted that the doctrine of Primacy is quite incontestable if you start from Universal ecclesiology. But even so, we can maintain a controversy with the Catholic Church, of the very highest importance; but only because primacy in the Church, according to Catholic theology, has no actual being unless it means the primacy of Rome. If there had been no Roman primacy, no other primacy could have existed; that is the Catholic view. Even granting that in fact the primacy did belong to Rome, such an admission of mere *fact* would not have been nearly enough for Catholic theologians: they might indeed have thought it more dangerous than a plain denial. Catholic theology requires us to admit the *dogmatic* assertion which says that primacy in the Church belongs solely to the See of Rome. But from another view, to deny the primacy of the Bishop of Rome does not necessarily involve denying the very idea of primacy. Far from it; so long as we stay in the sphere of universal ecclesiology, we must admit the idea of primacy in the Universal Church, though we should remember that the terms of stating it may be extremely varied. Oscar Cullmann is most significant on this subject: he resolutely rejects the dogmatic doctrine of the primacy of Rome, but still admits that primacy may exist in the Universal Church.[20] The Orthodox theologian Kartashev is of equal significance: he makes an equally categorical denial of the primacy of Rome, but has lately made a most resolute pronouncement in favor of the primacy of Constantinople within the bounds of the Orthodox Church.[21] Both affirmations witness that the doctrine of primacy derives, in a logical way, from a universal ecclesiology.

III

1. The influence of universal ecclesiology is so strong that it seems to theologically-minded people the only possible approach—almost an ec-

20 O. Cullmann, *Saint Pierre, disciple-apôtre-martyr* (Neuchâtel and Paris, 1952), pp. 213–15.
21 A. Kartashev, "La réunion de l'Orthodoxie" (in Russian), in *Tserkovnyi Vestnik* (1956) no. 5–6, pp. 4–12.

clesiological category without which any thought about the Church seems impossible. If universal ecclesiology is the only conceivable form, it must have been there from the beginning: but this line of argument will lead us to carry back our ecclesiology into a period when it really did not exist, and a whole string of anachronisms will inevitably follow, distorting the perspectives of history. Universal ecclesiology, however, is *not* the only one; what is more, it is not primitive ecclesiology, but quite the reverse: it has taken the place of a different ecclesiology, which I call eucharistic.

To begin with, I will recall a historical fact: in the apostolic age, and throughout the second and third centuries, every local church was autonomous and independent—autonomous, for it contained in itself everything necessary to its life; and independent, because it did not depend on any other local church or any bishop whatever outside itself. We ought not to regard this autonomy and independence just as a historical fact, due to chance or to the defects of church organization, then in its infancy—defects that disappeared when the organization took better shape and was more clearly defined. The development did in fact occur; but it does not follow that the organization of the primitive church was defective. In the subsequent history of church organization there was indeed a change, a change of underlying axiom: in other words, the doctrine of the Church (which gave the axioms of church organization) suffered change. Of course you can always deny the historical fact itself, or see it as a myth, but only at the price of setting *a priori* concepts above historical realities.

Well, if the autonomy and independence of primitive local churches were not due to chance, how can we account for them? If we begin with a universal ecclesiology, we can do nothing at all: one part of the Church—in this system, a local church—cannot possibly be autonomous or independent, for autonomy and independence are attributes of a whole. Therefore, the primitive churches were autonomous and independent in virtue of the fact that each local church was the Church of God in all its fullness. This conception of the nature of the local church implies the existence of an ecclesiological system, from which the concept of the Universal Church (at least in its existing form) is absent. And without this concept, the Universal Church cannot be mentioned at all.

2. We would never have found the idea of the Universal Church in the New Testament, and least of all in St Paul's writings, if it had not already been present in our minds. I cannot pause here to analyze the New Testament texts referring to the Church and show that they do not contain the concept of the Universal Church. The task would be elaborate and would only lead to arguments about the interpretation of this or that text. I think it will be more useful if I confine myself to explaining the main principles of eucharistic ecclesiology, a subject on which I have had frequent occasion to speak.

"You are the Body of Christ" (1 Cor 12:27). When the Apostle Paul wrote to tell the Corinthians that they were the Body of Christ, he surely cannot have helped thinking of the liturgical formula, "This is my Body," which he quotes in the same epistle. Scholars even now disagree about the sense in which "Body" (σῶμα) should be taken in St Paul—the Pauline sense is still difficult and open to discussion—but a comparative study of the two formulas gives us the key to St Paul's ecclesiology. "This is my Body" was the eucharistic formula received by Paul from the Church at Jerusalem; it was spoken every time that the "Lord's Supper" was celebrated. Even if it was not actually *spoken* in the Church of Jerusalem (which is most unlikely), it was certainly in the minds of all who shared in the Supper. When the Eucharist is celebrated, the bread becomes the Body of Christ, and by the bread the partakers become the Body of Christ. "The bread which we break, is it not a communion in the Body of Christ? Because there is one bread, we who are many are one body, for we all partake of the one bread" (1 Cor 10:16–17). The close tie between the loaf of bread and the Body of Christ comes out very clearly here. It is hard to see how "body" in Paul's "You are the body of Christ" (1 Cor 12:27) could mean anything different in 1 Cor 10:16–17. The local church—though "many" and "you" in the texts quoted above—is the Body of Christ in its eucharistic aspect. This conclusion is, to start with, obviously of the highest importance for its bearing on the doctrine of the Eucharist: the eucharistic bread is, here, the real Body of Christ. But it is also important with regard to the doctrine of the Church. Every "local" church is the Church of God in Christ, for Christ dwells in His Body in the congregation at the Eucharist, and the faithful become members of His Body by virtue of communicating in the Body of Christ. The indivisibility of Christ's Body implies the fullness of the Church dwelling in each of the "local" churches. This view of the Church is expressed in another of Paul's formulas: "the Church of God which *is* (or dwells) at Corinth," or anywhere else local churches are to be found.

To return to a point mentioned before: the local church is autonomous and independent, because the Church of God in Christ indwells it in perfect fullness. It is independent, because any power, of any kind, exercised over it would be exercised over Christ and His Body. It is autonomous, because fullness of being belongs to the Church of God in Christ, and outside it nothing is, for nothing can have being outside Christ.

At first sight, this eucharistic doctrine may look paradoxical, but the paradox does not attach to the Church; it is in our own empirical consciousness. The fact is that a large number of local churches *do* exist, in empirical reality, as they did in the days of the Apostles. Does this mean that *one* Church cannot exist, only a *number* of Churches of God in Christ? The impossibility of such a conclusion is absolutely clear: there cannot be a plurality of Churches of God in Christ, for Christ is one, and unique. We cannot very well apply Euclidean arithmetic, since ecclesiology works with quantities that cannot be reckoned up. "One plus one is two" is something we are used to in empirical consciousness, but where ecclesiology is concerned, to add up the local churches would be a waste of time. We should always have a total no larger than each item of the addition sum. "One plus one is still *one*" in ecclesiology. Every local church manifests all the fullness of the Church of God, because it *is* the Church of God and not just one part of it. There may be a plurality of such manifestations, but the Church of God itself always remains one and unique, for it always equals itself. Perhaps this is the time for me to repeat what I have had occasion to write elsewhere:

> Every local church enjoys all the fullness of the Church of God in Christ. The plurality of local churches does not destroy the unity of the Church of God, just as the plurality of eucharistic assemblies does not destroy the unity of the Eucharist in time and space. In the Church, unity and plurality are not only overcome: the one also contains the other. The unity of the Church in its empirical life is manifested by a plurality of local churches, and the plurality of the local churches safeguards the unity of the Church of God in Christ. If the

number of local churches is increased or diminished, the Church's unity and fullness remain unchanged; there will just be a variation in the number of its manifestations in empirical existence. This number of manifestations of the Church makes up its exterior universality and at the same time marks out the boundaries of the Church's earthly mission. And so eucharistic ecclesiology in no way rejects the universality of the Church but makes a distinction between exterior universality (in so far as the mission is limited), and interior universality, which equals itself always and in all circumstances, because it means that the Church manifests itself everywhere, always in fullness and unity.[22]

Thus the Church's fullness and unity are not a matter of quantity, but depend on the fullness and unity of the Body of Christ, who is always and everywhere one and unique in His fullness. Christ is always the same, yesterday, today, and forever, to one isolated church and to all local churches as well. Eucharistic ecclesiology teaches that the unity and fullness of the Church attach to the notion of a local church, and not to the fluid and indefinite notion of the Universal Church. The Eucharist is where Christ dwells in the fullness of His Body: the Eucharist could never have been offered in a local church if it had been no more than one part of the Church of God. Where the Eucharist is, there is the fullness of the Church; *vice versa*, where the fullness of the Church is not, there no Eucharist can be celebrated. By denying the idea of "parts," eucharistic ecclesiology also excludes any concept of the Universal Church, for the Universal Church consists of parts, if it exists at all.

3. We have already noticed above that the concept of "Universal Church" carries with it the idea of primacy; that is to say, the Universal Church must have a single bishop at its head. This "leadership" holds the reins of power over the Universal Church, although the leader is not above the Church but remains within its borders. An essential part of "universalist" teaching must always be the building up of this power as a legal principle, in the Church, whether the power is absolute or limited. But now we come to a new question—does eucharistic ecclesiology carry with it an idea of primacy? If so, what is its form and content?

Theologians were formerly interested in discussing whether the primitive local church had a single person at its head (it hardly matters what name he was called by), or whether one-man management was a feature of the second stage in the history of the church organization. I cannot

22 "L'apôtre Pierre et l'évêque de Rome," *Theologia* XXVI (Athens, 1955), pp. 11–12.

deal here with the historical side of the problem, and in any case it is difficult to solve, as direct information is lacking. But I would like to point out that, from an ecclesiological point of view, there can be no doubt that the local churches did have a single person as leader from the very beginning. Eucharistic ecclesiology has its own pattern of thought, in which "being head of a local church" means "being head" of the eucharistic assembly. The Last Supper was not the Eucharist, but only its institution. It became the Eucharist when Christ's disciples began to celebrate it in the breaking of bread and the blessing of the cup. Yet the Eucharist is not a repetition of the Supper: that, like the sacrifice on Golgotha, was accomplished "once for all." The Eucharist is a prolongation of the Supper in one special regard: it is an ecclesiological Last Supper, the "feast of the Lord" celebrated in the Church, by whose celebration the Church has being. As in Jewish meals, which served as models for the Last Supper, so in the Eucharist one person must preside. On the day of Pentecost at Jerusalem, the Eucharist was celebrated for the first time, and one of the disciples must have presided—it was certainly Peter. From that time onwards there was always one special person at the Eucharist who broke the bread and blessed the cup. The head of the eucharistic assembly was also the head of the local church, that manifestation of the Church of God whose Head is Christ.

Who is leader of the multitude of churches, and how are they governed in actual fact? Would one local church, or perhaps its bishop, stand as head over all the rest? This sort of question makes us wonder if primacy can really exist in the Church alongside the thought-patterns of eucharistic ecclesiology. Before answering this, we must see what the multitude of local churches represents. If we were guided by our empirical consciousness, we should have been forced to picture this multitude as being in dispersion, since each local church was independent and autonomous. But the categories of empirical consciousness cannot apply in this matter. The multitude of local churches was *not* dispersed, it was united. The union was something absolutely *sui generis*: the unity was not the result of separate parts reuniting, but it was the unity of one and the same Church. Each local church united in itself all the local churches because it possessed all the fullness of the Church of God, and all the local churches together were united, because they were always this same

Church of God. Though a local church did contain everything it needed within itself, it could not live apart from the other churches. It could not shut itself in or refuse to be acquainted with happenings in other churches: for anything that happened in other churches, as well as in its own, happened in the Church of God, the one and only Church. All the multitude of local churches forms one union founded on concord and love. Every local church must be in concord with all the other churches, because within the Church of God, ever one and only one, there can be no discord. This means, empirically speaking, that every local church accepts and makes its own anything that happens in other churches, and that all the churches accept everything that happens in each fellow-church. This acceptance (its regular designation is the word *reception* or *receptio*) is the witness of a local church indwelt by the Church of God, witnessing the work being done in other churches also indwelt by the Church of God—the Spirit bearing witness of the Spirit. By accepting what is being done in another church, one or several local churches bear witness that their actions are conformed to the will of God, and are therefore being done in the Church of God in Christ. Rejection of what is being done in a church, however, bears witness that such an action does not conform with the will of God.

The witness of local churches might vary in weight. In absolute terms, however, every local church has the same value as another. This equality of value is between the Church of God and herself; for she is one, unique, and fully present in the eucharistic assembly of every local church. If the local churches were not equal in value, we should have to say that the Church of God was not equal to itself in value. But there is no need to think that equality of value between local churches destroys the hierarchy of these churches, far from it: the equality creates a hierarchy of churches grounded in the authority of witness belonging to the several local churches. The Church of God lives fully present in the eucharistic assembly of the local churches, but each of them has a different way and degree of making the presence actual in its own life. A local church will have higher authority of witness if it has a greater realization of the presence of the Church of God. Though the local churches are by nature equal in value, they are not necessarily equal in authority: this difference in authority causes hierarchy among them. If there is a hierarchy of churches, there must also be a church to head the hierarchy—therefore, a church that takes the first place. Its act of bearing witness to events in other churches has a sovereign value, and its act of "reception" is of decisive importance. To put it another way, this church holds a two-fold priority, of authority and love, which means it makes a sacrificial gift of itself to the others. If the priority is of this nature we cannot possibly say that a church which possesses priority has *power* over the other churches. It never possessed or could possess power, for the power of a church having priority over the others would mean power over the Body of Christ. One cannot even say that the primacy was one of honor, for in ancient times the ideas of honor and power were closely associated. What is more, there was nothing honorific about priority in the hierarchy of churches, in the modern sense of the word: the church that came first among the local churches won its place by services rendered, and not by prestige. It could not impose its will on the other churches or make them carry out its decisions, for all decisions must first be ratified by other local churches. Another point to notice: even in the period of ecumenical councils, and in spite of a system of church order which was quite different from what it had been before Nicaea, no one church or group of churches had power over the others, in any strict sense of the word. If one of the churches did not recognize some doctrine as a manifestation of the will of God, no one could force it to do so. Even the imperial power, though it possessed the means to constrain, was often powerless in such matters. Thus it came about that one church gradually drew away from the main flock into a separate fold (by itself or with other churches who had the same ideas), and this fold was considered as heretical or schismatic by the other churches, because it had refused the witness of the church-in-priority and of other churches in concord with the leading one.

The church-in-priority had no power, and no special rights either: the many churches were not joined by law, but by love and concord. That is why a single church surrounded by many concordant churches only increases in authority by a corresponding increase in love. The church that had priority naturally possessed the highest degree of authority, together with the greatest love, and would always be ready to come to the help of churches in need. Dionysius of Corinth says in a letter to Pope Soter:

Your custom [at Rome] has been from the beginning to do good to your brethren in various ways, and send succor to numerous churches in every city: thus, you have comforted the nakedness of the indigent, and you have sustained our brethren in the mines by the help you sent from the very first. You [Romans] are keeping the old Roman tradition, which your blessed Bishop Soter not only preserves but even enhances, by the abundant provision and help that he sends to the saints, and also by consoling the brethren who come to him with words of cheer, like a kind father who loves to do his children good.[23]

The basis of priority is neither power, nor honor, but only the authority that flows from love and is made manifest by love. The church-in-priority may make mistakes in the very act of coming to the rescue of churches in need and especially of churches in error; that is why the witness of the other churches is needed. Its grand mistake is wanting to impose a sovereign will or put itself above other churches. This is the first step that leads in the end to revoking priority and resisting the will of God, for it is a renouncing of the love that spreads throughout the Church. By putting itself above all the number of local churches, which embosom its own priority, it takes a road that may lead it outside the bounds of that number, to a place where there is no priority, only a realm of "ecclesiological vacuum." Priority implies the existence of a number of local churches, and every church among them is the Church of God just as much as the is church-in-priority. When a local church invokes the church-in-priority, it is not invoking judgment from a tribunal against which there is no appeal, but coming to the church-in-priority so as to find itself, by hearing the voice of the Church which dwells there.

A hierarchy of churches, based on authority of witness, implies that the churches which form the hierarchy and are led by the church-in-priority all have full ecclesiastical *esse*; but it further implies that other churches will have priority in the small circles of local churches. This means that the church-in-priority possesses the highest authority, but not the sole authority; the other churches in their lower places in the hierarchy have their own authority, and neither kind excludes the other.

What possible explanation can we give for the priority of one church among the whole number of local churches? You may explain it, to be sure, by her own endeavors to manifest in her own life the Church of God in Christ, on the basis of purely historical facts—her being in some

23 Eusebius, *Hist. Eccl.* IV, xxiii, 10.

special town, or being founded by Apostles, or having many adherents—
but all these causes are not sufficient in themselves, since other local
churches may perfectly well possess whatever advantages the church-in-
priority possesses. It must be admitted in the end that priority is a gift of
God, and so an election by God. We cannot fully understand it, but the
whole mass of local churches accept it in freedom and love, and follow
the church-in-priority.

We may now return to a former enquiry: does the eucharistic type of
ecclesiology include the idea of primacy, or not? After all we have said
about it, clearly the only possible answer is negative: eucharistic ecclesiology excludes the idea of primacy by its very nature. As we already
know, primacy means the power of one bishop over the whole universal
Church. Such a power cannot exist in the eyes of eucharistic ecclesiology,
or (to be exact) this power cannot pass beyond the bounds enclosing a
local church. Conversely, as we have already seen, the local churches
appear to the eyes of eucharistic ecclesiology not as separated or divided;
not at all, they are mutually joined together. One of them occupies a very
special position, and so finds itself head of the other churches. In
describing this state of affairs I prefer to use the word "priority," and not
the word "primacy." Such a terminological nicety may seem very artificial, but it is justified because the concept of primacy is so enormously
different from the concept of priority; indeed, either concept almost
excludes the other. In eucharistic ecclesiology, priority belongs to one of
the local churches; but the concept of primacy, in its historical shape and
setting, assumes that primacy belongs to one of the bishops, and that he
governs the whole Church by established right. Consequently, primacy
is a legalistic expression, whereas priority is founded on authority of
witness, and that is a gift God grants to the church-in-priority. Of course
the priority of a church is reflected in the person of its bishop, but
eucharistic ecclesiology would consider his priority to be a secondary
phenomenon; universal ecclesiology holds that a bishop's primacy is an
essential phenomenon. Throughout history, the primacy of a bishop has
always been tied to some definite church, but we may admit *theoretically*
that the person who possesses primacy might be found altogether outside
any definite church; certain trends in Catholic thought prove it. Finally,
we should note that the two concepts imply different doctrines of

Church unity: the "primacy" school attributes the unity to the Church universal, while those who uphold "priority" say that every local church has it. The difference between the concepts (primacy and priority) is very important: if you accept the idea of primacy you must ban eucharistic ecclesiology; conversely, accept the notion of priority and there is no room for universal ecclesiology.

IV

1. As I said before, if people transpose the universal ecclesiology of today into a time before it existed, they will create an inaccurate picture of church life in the ancient world. They will set problems unknown to that period, and unanswerable by our learning. For this reason, I must now turn to consider a few historical facts in the light of eucharistic ecclesiology. In surveying the horizon of history, I hope, incidentally, to find the chance to show that eucharistic ecclesiology is not based on abstract theological speculation, unrelated to live reality, but can be deduced from the Church's own history.

The historical analysis will be restricted, partly because lack of space in the present work is a limitation, but even more because eucharistic ecclesiology gradually gave way to universal ecclesiology, from the second half of the third century onwards.

2. According to universal ecclesiology, the Church had a single personal Head, chosen by Christ as soon as its life began. Can we find any historical proof that such a person ever existed, and was he the Apostle Peter, as Catholic theologians assert? If the Apostle Peter was not the leader of the Church, we are forced to conclude that the Catholic doctrine of primacy has no ecclesiological roots, was formed gradually in the course of history, and cannot therefore be regarded as a dogmatic obligation. A further question in this connection, still more important for Catholics, is the succession after Peter. If Peter had no successors, the whole doctrine of primacy would be undermined.

But we must also pose yet another question: is the primacy of Peter a problem we can properly discuss? As a matter of fact, such a problem never arose in the mind of the primitive Church. The first Christians were not concerned to discuss who was head of the Church, or, in concrete terms, whether or not Peter was its head; it was no problem to them because they had no need at all to ask this kind of question. The first Christians were as yet innocent of the very idea that there could be a power over the local churches, let alone discussing whether this power belonged to an individual, whether a Church or an Apostle, whether Jerusalem, Antioch, or Rome. The issue simply never crossed their minds.

The primacy of Peter has its premises in the statement "When Christ founded the Church, He had the Universal Church in view." To say the least, the statement is scarcely capable of being demonstrated; furthermore, the whole Pauline doctrine of the Church is against it. Cyprian of Carthage was the first person who voiced the idea that Mt 16:17-19 is a text about the Universal Church. Admittedly, we can find pointers to this *logion* of Christ as early as Justin (though he only comments on verse 17)[24]—but neither Justin, nor Irenaeus, nor Tertullian so much as asked the question, or even wanted to know if the passage referred to the Universal Church: to them, the idea of a Universal Church was non-existent. Even granting that the statement is true, that Mt 16:18 ought to be taken to mean that Christ promised to build His Church on Peter, does this mean that Christ has placed Peter at the head of "His Church"? We cannot draw that conclusion, and would never have done so unless the idea of a Universal Church had been in our minds already. What is more, such a conclusion would make the *logion* itself appear a trifle illogical. If Peter really is the rock on which the Church is built, how can he be the chief of the Church at the same time? Insofar as Peter is the rock on which the Church is built, his role is passive: the Church is built on Peter by Christ, not by Peter.[25] The only grounds for giving Peter power over the Church might be found in Christ's promise to give him "the keys of the Kingdom of Heaven." "The keys," of course, can be seen as a different thing from "binding and loosing"; but in the *logion* itself the "power of the keys" is not the point. We shall not find the promised "power of the keys" in our *logion* unless, I repeat, we take our start from an assumed idea of the Universal Church.

We will now leave aside all the familiar difficulties that arise in

24 J. Ludwig, *Die Primatwörte Mt xvi. 18, 19 in der altkirchlichen Exegese* (Munster, W.), p. 7.
25 P. Bonnard, *Jésus-Christ édifiant son Eglise* (Neuchâtel and Paris, 1948), p. 26.

interpreting Mt 16:18, and will allow that Christ made Peter head of the Church by these words. If this had been the case, then the primacy of Peter would certainly have become clear and manifest in the course of early church history. Yet the relevant historical facts in this period are far from proving it so. There is a great deal we do not know about apostolic times, but surely the Church's memory cannot have failed to preserve what was most important. A study of Acts will provide us with one incontestable conclusion: Peter *was* the head of the Church of Jerusalem, which was a local church, although it was for a time the only church; when other local churches grew up, James, the brother of the Lord, became chief of the Church of Jerusalem. We do not know if Peter was head of some other church at the time. In supporting the primacy of Peter, we should have to say that he exerted his primacy independently, without connection with any local church—a quite impossible assertion to make, either about those days or about any other. We see, then, that the primacy of Peter was not plainly manifested in the primitive church, and that we cannot positively assert the fulfillment of the promise given to Peter, at least not if we understand it as a promise of primacy. We are faced here with riddles that we are unable to answer, and the reason for the riddles is that we stated the problem badly.

3. If we take eucharistic ecclesiology for our starting-point, many of the riddles can be answered without much difficulty. In that case we must not ask whether Peter was head of the Church. The interesting question now is, which local church had the priority in that period; or rather, did any church have priority during the apostolic age? Eucharistic ecclesiology would seem to imply so. Apparently no one contests the special place held by the Church of Jerusalem until the death of James, brother of the Lord; it only remains to see what kind of place it held. Is Bishop Cassian right in his assertion that the Church of Jerusalem constituted the hierarchical center during the primitive period, or anyhow until the city fell, and that the other churches lived under its jurisdiction?[26] The phraseology does not matter, since the writer is speaking the language of convention. What we really want to know is whether the Church of Jerusalem had *power* over the others. In the time

26 Bishop Cassian, "Saint-Pierre et l'Eglise dans le Nouveau Testament (le problème de la
    Primauté)," *Istina* (1955/3) 262-4.

of famine, under the emperor Claudius, the Church of Antioch sent help to the Church of Jerusalem by the good offices of Barnabas and Saul (Acts 11:30). Luke thought it his duty to record this, which was very likely the first occasion when one church sent help to another: the first, but not the last—the story of the ancient church abounds with similar examples. Whether or not the Church of Antioch was dependent on Jerusalem, this move of theirs was an expression of the love uniting all the churches. No doubt they would have done the same for any other church that might have needed help. The Apostle Paul lays particular stress on collecting offerings for the poor, to benefit the Church of Jerusalem. This collection has been endlessly discussed by theological writers. It is highly dubious—in fact utterly improbable—that Paul saw in it a sort of Christian "two drachmae" payable to the Christian Jerusalem. Even if he did, we still have no reason to infer that the local churches, in Palestine or outside, thought themselves in any way subject to the power of the church at Jerusalem. It is common knowledge that the power of the Sanhedrin did not extend to the Jewish *diaspora*; its authority was purely of a moral and religious kind. Paul collected his contributions because the people were moved by a loving impulse and a desire to help the needy, especially those of the Church of Jerusalem. Another point struck Paul even more strongly: he thought this piece of charity was visible proof that the Jewish-Christian and Gentile-Christian churches were at one. The theological significance of these collections is therefore unquestionable.[27]

The facts I have just explained prove the special character of the place held by the Church of Jerusalem. To define this, we must begin with the presuppositions that were accepted in the apostolic age, and set aside all modern assumptions. This brings us to the following definition: after local churches had grown up, in Palestine and also beyond its borders, the Church of Jerusalem had a position of priority among them. It possessed priority by virtue of being the church most authoritative in witnessing. This place of honor is easy to understand: from Pentecost onwards, Jerusalem was the first place where the Church of God in Christ took shape, and the building up of the local churches began from Jerusalem. There Christ suffered and rose again, there for some while they expected His second coming, and there was the dwelling-place of the Apostles. All

27 J. Munck, *Paulus und die Heilsgeschichte* (Copenhagen, 1954), pp. 286ff.

this made a halo of special glory round Jerusalem, and the Jewish-Christians were not alone in seeing it—the Gentile Christians saw it too. There was no other church that could be compared to Jerusalem, and so its witness had the most authority. Any disagreement with Jerusalem amounted almost to deviation from the true faith, and agreement carried a corresponding guarantee of soundness. No wonder the Apostle Paul found it necessary to explain to Jerusalem what sort of gospel he was preaching to the Gentiles; it was the only way he could find out if "his race was run in vain" (Gal 2:2). His action was no sort of appeal to a higher court, a court possessed of the power to license or prohibit Paul's missionary activities. If the Church of Jerusalem had been a hierarchical center, Paul would have needed to get its authorization in advance, a thing that he never dreamed of asking. When Paul applied to the Church of Jerusalem (represented by "those of most reputation"), he wanted them to bear witness to the truth and authenticity of his gospel. Paul himself says nothing about his motives for doing this, and speaks only of a revelation: "I went up [to Jerusalem] by revelation; and I laid before them (but privately before those who were of repute) the gospel which I preach among the Gentiles" (Gal 2:2). Nevertheless, if we are to be guided by what we find in Acts, we could suppose that Paul applied to the Church of Jerusalem after, and because of, the conflict that had taken place at Antioch, when doubts had been expressed as to whether Paul's doctrine was the truth. Acceptance of his gospel by the Church of Jerusalem gave witness that it was true. We can say, in short, that Paul applied to the church which possessed the greatest authority, and the Church of Jerusalem behaved as a church-with-priority.

Paul undoubtedly recognized that the Church of Jerusalem had supreme authority in matters of witness; but this recognition, to him, did not oblige him to feel dependent on the Church of Jerusalem in respect to his personal action, or in respect to the churches he had founded. When Paul looks back on his visits to Jerusalem in the Epistle to the Galatians, he makes it clear that he does not depend on the Church of Jerusalem in his apostolic activity. I think it is very unlikely that Paul believed he had to go to Jerusalem in order to give them an account of his missionary journeys.[28] The visit spoken of in Gal 2:1-10 was inspired by other motives, as we know. As for his last journey to Jerusalem, all we

28 Bishop Cassian, p. 263.

know is that Paul wanted to deliver personally the assistance he had brought for their poor to the Church of Jerusalem.

The sources give us no reason to suppose that Paul was in a dependent relation to Jerusalem; nor do they give us ground for asserting that the Church of Jerusalem ever claimed to extend her power over the Pauline churches or over Paul himself. Whatever conflicts there were, if any, between Paul and the Church of Jerusalem, and particularly with James, one thing is beyond question. There was a strong opposition party within that Church, and it became stronger still after Paul's *concordat* with the "Pillars" (Gal 2:9). If the Church of Jerusalem really had any power over Paul, the members of the opposition could have tried to obtain a clearly worded decision against him. At any rate, the "Judaizers"—whether sent by James, or by the Church of Jerusalem—did not behave like people who have been given a definite mandate. When a church or a personage invests people with the power that a mission implies, they do not behave as the "Judaizers" did.[29] One further point must be added to these remarks, and it concerns ecclesiology. Even if Jerusalem had possessed universal jurisdiction, it could not have reached beyond the churches and their bishops; it could not cover individual Christians, who were dependent on their several churches; otherwise we should have to suppose that there were no churches outside the Church of Jerusalem, and this was not the case. Paul could not be dependent on the Church of Jerusalem; he was never a member of it. As an apostle, he could not be dependent on the Church of Jerusalem, either; for his apostolate was, in his own words "not of men neither by man." He was like the other apostles in never being bishop of a church founded by himself. The theory of the apostle-bishop, so widely accepted in Catholic and even non-Catholic circles, is the product of theological speculation: the object is to prove that the monarchical episcopate was there from the beginning. The primitive churches saw an *episcopus* as presiding over a single local church, not over a group of them. Paul was admittedly the head-figure to the churches he founded; even so, he cannot have been the *episcopus* of so many all at once.

It is equally bad ecclesiology to ask the question: was the Apostle Peter

29 The "Judaizers" were connected in various ways with the Church of Jerusalem; or perhaps we should follow Munck in supposing that they were former Gentiles converted to Christianity.

dependent on the Church of Jerusalem? I confess that, for me, the problem of Peter's primacy seems to be a false problem; but the problem of Peter himself is real. I cannot possibly tackle the subject at present, or I should wander too far from the immediate point under review. It is enough simply to say that Peter stood in a place apart among the apostles, and that his ministry was unique in kind and had no later parallels. The Apostle Peter is the rock on which the Church is built, and will remain the rock until the coming of the Lord. But Peter's place and his apostolic ministry could never have set him outside the Church's boundaries. Another thing to note: belonging to the Church is concrete, not abstract—that is, you cannot belong to the Church in general, you have to belong to one church in particular: the Church of God is manifested as empirical reality in the local churches. This concrete way of belonging to a local church implies a relation of dependence upon it, though we should be careful to avoid describing this dependency in modern terms of law and jurisdiction, for grace is its foundation. The dependence is really on the will of God, who rules the Church's life. In the early days of the Church of Jerusalem, the Apostle Peter was its head; this did not make him independent in regard to the Church, for in that case he could not have functioned as its head. Conversely, the Church of Jerusalem depended, to some extent, on Peter as being its head. During this phase of Peter's life, his course of action had to run parallel to the action of the Church of Jerusalem, in full concord. So there is no surprise in the fact that, after his missionary journey and the conversion of Cornelius, Peter reported about them to the Jerusalem church assembly. How could he possibly withhold such an amazing story from them: an uncircumcised pagan received into the Church (for the first time, according to the Acts)! When they heard these things (that is, after hearing Peter's account) they held their peace and glorified God, saying: "Then to the Gentiles also God has granted repentance unto life" (Acts 11:18). Here was an example of the Church of Jerusalem bearing witness about the will of God, and submitting (the Church, not Peter alone) to God's will. Legal submission (i.e., to a qualified authority) belongs to quite a different world, and Luke's story makes no mention of it. We know almost nothing about St Peter's doings after he left Jerusalem; but we can state with a high degree of probability that, whatever St Peter was doing, he was not dependent on the Church of Jerusalem, at least in a legalistic sense, and least of all as an apostle of Christ. If he had been dependent, we should have had to ask how and where his dependency could find concrete expression. After the "Apostolic Council" which Peter attended, as Acts recounts, he never came to Jerusalem again, so he cannot have participated in the Jerusalem church assembly. We are left with the supposition—most unlikely—that Peter sent in regular reports to Jerusalem. Still another hypothesis is suggested by O. Cullmann in his book on St Peter: Peter was dependent not on the Church of Jerusalem but on St James in person, because he was the head of the Christian-Jewish mission.[30] This notion rests on the supposition that St James was actually the head of the Universal Church. But that is a highly questionable hypothesis, without any *data* to support it; and it led O. Cullmann to the conclusion that the Christian Jews, no matter where they might be situated, were always dependent on St Peter. According to O. Cullmann, in one self-same church, say the Church of Rome, some of the faithful were dependents of St Peter, and others looked elsewhere. Such a supposition is quite inadmissible, because it leaves out the idea of the Church.

4. After James died, and still more after Jerusalem fell in A.D. 70, the Church of Jerusalem ceased to play the part of leading church. It disappeared from the historical stage: when it made a new entrance it appeared as a small church in the new pagan city of Aelia Capitolina, and the congregation was entirely composed of Gentile Christians. So far had its prestige crumbled, that even in Palestine leadership had passed to the Church of Caesarea; surely this is still further proof that the Church of Jerusalem had not held the primacy before the year 70. Primacy in any case is inseparably bound up with a man, not with a church. If the primacy had belonged to James, he would have passed it over to his successors; men δεσπόσυνοι like himself, that is, kindred of Christ in the flesh. To whom, then, was the priority which formerly belonged to the Church of Jerusalem transferred? The New Testament scriptures give us no guidance on this point, and so we have to look for an answer in the facts of history, and the premises of ecclesiology. If the local churches were gathered round one authoritative church in the beginning, why were they to do without such a center later on? We can strongly assert

30 O. Cullmann, pp. 37, 39.

that no church could have inherited Jerusalem's authority in full. The authority given to the Church of Jerusalem was unique and unrepeatable. True enough; but there is no need to ask whether another church could have inherited Jerusalem's authority in full. We are only concerned to discover which had most authority among the churches—if not so great as the primitive authority of Jerusalem, at least greater than the others could boast of.

Let us turn to the facts. We know that the Church of Rome took over the position of "church-with-priority" at the end of the first century. That was about the time at which her star ascended into the firmament of history in its brightest splendor. We cannot tell exactly when this happened, for there was never a formal transmission of priority from Jerusalem to Rome. Even as early as the Epistle to the Romans, Rome seems to have stood out among all the churches as very important. Paul bears witness that the faith of the Romans was proclaimed throughout the whole world (Rom 1:8). The persecutions of Nero did not reduce the Church of Rome to nothing, but it was so badly damaged that some period of time was needed to arouse its spirit and collect its numerical strength. In the time of this transition, as we should expect, it could not play the part of the leading church. We do not know who held the priority during this comparatively short period: it may possibly have been Antioch, which stood in an important ecclesiastical position even in the time of St James. It may have been Ephesus, though this is less likely, for that church's influence never spread beyond Asia Minor. If Ephesus had really possessed the priority then, surely it would have had possession at the end of the first century. However, we have a document which gives us our earliest reliable evidence that the Church of Rome stood in an exceptional position of authority in this period. This is the epistle of Clement of Rome. Modern theological scholars (especially Protestants) regard Clement of Rome as a name intimately associated with the beginnings of pre-Catholicism, or even of Catholicism at Rome. This is one of the great axioms to be found in modern theological learning, those formulas potent as magic spells, even when totally groundless. We know that Clement was "president" of the Roman Church: that is all. G. Dix, writing to defend the theory of apostle-bishops, considered that Clement was the heir and successor of the Apostles Peter and Paul in exactly the same way as (he thinks) Timothy and Titus had been. In other words, Clement is supposed to have been the bishop of a considerable number of churches, which were governed by presbyteries. This opinion belongs in a world of pure fantasy, and will not stand up to serious critical investigation.[31]

The epistle is not written by Clement alone; but in the name of the Roman Church. "The Church of God dwelling in Rome to the Church of God dwelling in Corinth." This form of address already proves that the Roman Church did not set itself above the Church of Corinth; they are both called "Church of God." There is no hint in the epistle of any claim being made by the Church of Rome to exercise any power over the Church of Corinth. If the Church of Rome had believed itself to be invested with a higher power, then the Epistle of Clement would surely have been written in a very different tone. We do not know exactly what had happened at Corinth; the epistle only mentions a "rebellion" against the presbyters, which had led to the presbyters' (or rather, one presbyter's) being ejected. This presbyter was the head of the Church, that is, he was the bishop. We again do not know by what means the news of these events had reached Rome. It is easy to suppose that the presbyter or presbyters thus ejected applied to the Church of Rome. But could they have thought Rome had the power to annul their ejection? This is most unlikely; the establishment or ejection of presbyters was the business of a local church. The real reason they applied to the Roman Church was that Rome might refuse to recognize the recent decisions made in the Church of Corinth; might refuse *receptio* of what had taken place in the Church of Corinth. The Church of Rome did that very thing: bore witness that the ejected presbyters had done nothing amiss, and said that their deposition was not in accordance with the will of God. This was not Rome laying down the law, but the Church bearing witness about what had happened within the Church. The epistle is couched in very measured terms, in the form of an exhortation; but at the same time it clearly shows that the Church of Rome was aware of the decisive weight, in the Church of Corinth's eyes, that must attach to its witness about the events in Corinth. So the Church of Rome, at the end of the first century, exhibits a marked sense of its own priority, in point

31 G. Dix, "The Ministry in the Early Church," in *The Apostolic Ministry* (1946), pp. 253–66.

of witness about events in other churches. Note also that the Roman Church did not feel obliged to make a case, however argued, to justify its authoritative pronouncements on what we should now call the internal concerns of other churches. There is nothing said about the grounds of this priority; even though the text of the epistle mentions the Apostles Peter and Paul and their death under Nero's persecution, and one might well expect this to have been enlarged upon as affording a foundation for Roman priority. Apparently Rome had no doubt that its priority would be accepted without argument. The only apology made is for not having sent a letter to the Church of Corinth earlier, so as to restore order there, the delay being due to persecutions.

5. We do not know if the Corinthian Church followed Rome's advice, but we may fairly suppose that the voice of the Roman Church was heard. Anyhow, Clement's epistle was held in high esteem at Corinth thereafter. This is an interesting fact, but it still does not prove that Rome's priority was recognized by other churches. Our next task, therefore, is to find out were what the views of other churches. We find the first direct evidence about the priority of the Roman Church in the writings of Ignatius of Antioch. Speaking of the Church of Rome, Ignatius uses the phrase "which presides" in two passages. "Ignatius also named Theophoros...to the church which presides in the land of the Romans...which presides in love (ἀγάπη)."[32] The term *agape* is the hardest part of the passage to explain, but the difficulty vanishes if we take into account the special meaning Ignatius gave to *agape*: for him, *agape* meant "the local church in its eucharistic aspect." Each local church is *agape*: all local churches together are also *agape*, because each local church, says Ignatius, is the Catholic Church and so manifests the Church of God in Christ. In the empirical sphere, however, the churches form a union based on love, and this union may also be spoken of in the same words. The Roman Church "presides" in love, that is, in the concord based on love between all the local churches. The term "which presides" (προκαθημένη) needs no discussion; used in the masculine it means the bishop, for he, as head of the local church, sits in the "first place" at the eucharistic assembly, that is, in the central seat. He is truly

32 Romans. Salutation. Ignatius of Antioch, *Letters*, tr. P. T. Camelot in *Sources chrétiennes* 10 (Paris, 1951), p. 125.

the president of his church. Because a local church was by nature identical with the concord of all the churches in love, an image came naturally to Ignatius' mind: he pictured the local churches grouped, as it were, in a eucharistic assembly, with every church in its special place, and the Church of Rome in the chair, sitting in the "first place." So, says Ignatius, the Church of Rome indeed has the priority in the whole company of churches united by concord. We are not told by Ignatius (or by Clement, either) why the Church of Rome should preside, and not some other church. To Ignatius it must have seemed self-evident, and proofs a waste of time. In his period no other church laid claim to the role, which belonged to the Church of Rome. At the beginning of the second century, the Church of Alexandria had not yet appeared on the historical scene, but seemed to lurk in some mysterious shadow. As for the Church of Ephesus—Ignatius did indeed send them an epistle, but it does not contain the least allusion to their having any special role. The only important church after Rome was Antioch—they could have claimed leadership—but Ignatius himself attributes this role to Rome, although he is quite clear that great respect is due to his own church and to himself. It is enough to compare his epistle to the Church of Rome with the other Ignatian epistles; one immediately feels the difference of tone. In his other epistles he teaches like a doctor; but when addressing Rome, he does not venture to give any advice at all. Every line in this epistle is charged with special deference to "the church that presides in love."

Nevertheless, in the epistle to the Church of Rome, we find no reference to its power over the other churches, and Ignatius does not say anything about the Bishop of Rome. This is puzzling to us, but also proves that Ignatius had absolutely no idea of Roman primacy. Priority, to him, did not imply the notion of power. Priority must, of course, be so understood as to correspond with the way in which the local churches are understood. If every church's life is founded on love, if love underlies all relations with other churches, then priority too must spring from love and be a living example of love's authority. Ignatius almost certainly knew of Clement of Rome's epistle, in which the Church of Rome refused to countenance the ejection of Corinthian presbyters; but he had never heard of any standards laid down by the Church of Rome to regulate doctrine or discipline. If such standards existed, he would certainly have applied them to various issues, especially to his doctrine of bishops. He writes to the Romans: "As for you, you have been grudging to none, you have taught others. I can only wish that what you enjoin on others by your instructions may carry due weight."[33] But the words are used in a very limited sense. The reference is solely to moral issues, and here especially to envy, which had been the chief subject of Clement's epistle.

Ignatius, in another saying even harder to explain, says that the Church of Rome "presides in the region of the Romans" (προκαθῆται ἐν τόπῳ χωρίου ʿΡωμαίων). What does this mean? We can be sure that Ignatius was not talking here about the Roman Church presiding in Rome itself, for such an expression would be meaningless: a bishop can preside over a church, but a church cannot preside over itself. We must therefore suppose that Ignatius is talking about the Church of Rome's presidency among the local churches situated "in Roman country." We do not know what churches these were, but it is an established fact that other churches in central Italy did exist at the time of Ignatius. His words justify our supposing some kind of union between various Italian local churches; among them the Roman Church possessed the priority. If so, a further conclusion may be drawn: in the period of Ignatius of Antioch, besides the one great union of all local churches, more limited unions had come into being, groups of churches round one particular church which had the most authority. Such unions had arisen through the force of events. After all, it was not always either easy or essential to invoke Rome, with her then supreme priority. It was much simpler and more convenient to approach some less distant church, possessed of greater authority than her neighbors. Ecclesiastical hierarchy had always been there, ever since the churches first began. The church-in-priority certainly had authority, but this did not prevent a daughter-church from also having an authoritative position among churches lesser than itself; only, of course, its authority could not be so great. Ignatius regards Rome as the church-in-priority, and his witness on this point agrees with the Roman Church's self-witness, as we find it in the Epistle of Clement.

6. We shall find other evidence about the Roman position in Irenaeus, Bishop of Lyons. His *Adversus Haereses* contains a famous pas-

33 Rom 3:1.

sage, which has provoked a great many arguments. This is unquestionably the most important document of all with regard to the position of the Roman Church. The author is a father of the Church in the second half of the second century, a man who enjoyed very high prestige. The passage has come down to us in a Latin translation, and this makes it difficult to interpret in many places. I have chosen to quote the Latin because there is, so far, no generally accepted translation.

> Ad hanc enim ecclesiam propter potentiorem principalitatem necesse est omnem convenire ecclesiam, hoc est eos qui sunt undique fideles, in qua semper ab his qui sunt undique conservata est ea quae est ab apostolis traditi.[34]

This sentence has been discussed for centuries, almost word by word; but the most important point has never been discussed at all—nobody has asked whether Irenaeus was here talking about the Church of *Rome*. In other words, does the exordium *ad hanc enim ecclesiam* point to the Church of Rome? Till now all theologians, of every confession and trend, have agreed on assuming that the church in question was undoubtedly Rome. But Pierre Nautin challenged this consensus quite recently in his important article: "Irenaeus, *Adv. Haer.* III, 3, 2. Church of Rome or Church Universal."[35] In his opinion, Irenaeus is not talking about the Church of Rome, far from it; he means the Church Universal. A very original point of view this—even paradoxical. That a viewpoint is paradoxical does not necessarily commend it to our favor, but neither does it prove that the viewpoint is wrong, for truth often wears the guise of paradox, even in the field of theological inquiry. P. Nautin's article is very interesting, not only for its main thesis, which may be accepted or rejected as we please, but for the many fascinating observations it contains. I cannot of course linger over details now, but I must make up my mind for or against Nautin's main thesis. If he is right, and the passage in *Adv. Haer.* III, 3, 2, has nothing to do with the Church of Rome, then it has no further interest for me. And the remarkable thing is that the author of the article himself comes to the same conclusion; the famous passage loses its former importance to scholars under the light of his

34 The translation proposed by F. Sagnard (Irénée de Lyon, *Contre les Hérésies, Sources chrétiennes* 54, III, 3, 2 [Paris, 1952]) runs: "This Church [of Rome], by reason of being founded with more powerful authority, must command the concordance of every church with herself: that is, of the faithful who come from everywhere: she is in whom the tradition, coming from the Apostles, has always been preserved, by those who come from everywhere."
35 In *Revue de l'histoire des religions*, CLI/1 (January-March 1957).

interpretation; its content is now a platitudinous truth, i.e., every church should be in accord with the Church Universal.

Nautin's fundamental premises, which prove his interpretation of *Adv. Haer.* III, 3, 2, right or wrong, lie in the assertion that Irenaeus' ecclesiology was "universal." If this universal type of ecclesiology had not yet come into being in Irenaeus' time, Nautin's interpretation simply disintegrates; Irenaeus cannot have been talking about the Universal Church if the idea was foreign to his thought. Readers of the article might find all the arguments convincing, if only Nautin had given really clear proof that this idea of a Universal Church was in Irenaeus' mind from the start. We find no such proof in his article; he never even raises the question of what ecclesiology Irenaeus believed.

Let us suppose Nautin was right, and that the idea of a Universal Church can really be found in Irenaeus. If so, the sentence in question is no longer important and, worse still, the whole structure of Irenaeus' argument suffers the same fate. Irenaeus calls on apostolic tradition to correct the mistaken heretics. This tradition, he says, is guarded in every local church by the succession of bishops.[36] It was not in his power to find proof of this in each local church, so he confines himself to one set of bishops only, and enumerates the bishops of Rome, a church in which apostolic tradition and the faith proclaimed to mankind have been guarded up to his own times. This should be enough to confound those who set up irregular conventicles. This is the reason (says Nautin) why all churches, including those in heresy, must be in accord with the Universal Church, if they claim really to be churches. But if Irenaeus is truly discussing the Universal Church, how could he suppose that accord with it would seem to the heretics an argument against their own heterodoxy—or an argument to the faithful proving the apostolic tradition was true? What does "being in accord with the Universal Church" really mean? When we and our contemporaries say, and we often do, that the faithful should be in accord with the Church, we surely mean in accord with the doctrine preserved by the Church, as characterized and expressed in the symbols of the Faith, the decisions of ecumenical councils, the writings of the Church's fathers and the liturgical life. None of these things were there in the second century (or almost none); only the

36 *Adv. haer.* III, 3, 1.

Scripture and the tradition were preserved in each local church by the good offices of successive bishops. In the second century, to insist on accord with the Universal Church as a necessity is simply to pass from concrete to abstract: the concept of the Universal Church is itself an abstraction. Finally and essentially, any arguments against heretics based on the concept of the Universal Church really involve accepting the heretical attitude. The heretics could always reply that *their* doctrine was right and in accord with "the Church," that is, with the aeon "ecclesia" in their system of emanations. As for their attitude to Scripture and Tradition—go back to Irenaeus' own words:

> When we convict them by Scriptural proofs, they turn their attack upon the very Scriptures...Again, when we appeal to the Tradition, which comes from the Apostles, and is kept in the churches by the successions of presbyters, they reject that Tradition (III, 2, 1–2).

Irenaeus leaves no room for the opinion of P. Nautin; for if his sentence is taken to refer to the Universal Church, then it will appear absolutely isolated from its context.

I must confess that P. Nautin's arguments do not convince me. It seems to me that Irenaeus *was* referring to the Church of Rome in *Adv. Haer.* III, 3, 2, and that there can be no argument about this. I admit that some of his expressions remain a little obscure to us, and our interpretations are just hypotheses, some plausible and others not. But the general sense of the sentence is clear enough, at least for my own purposes.[37] As I showed above, Irenaeus believed he could confine himself to enumerating the succession in a single church, viz. the Roman Church, although he might have enumerated the successive bishops in every local church, as he says himself. He gives his own explanation for choosing the Church of Rome: he saw it as "the very great and the very ancient church, known to all, which the two most glorious apostles Peter and Paul founded and

---

37 I cannot here give a philological analysis of Irenaeus' sentence, not only because space is lacking. In fact, philological analysis of the sentence has so far given us nothing, and any future yield is doubtful. Turning the Latin back into Greek would be a hopeful line if one had a dictionary of Irenaeus' works. But in proposing our different translations, we shall never be sure that the original text has really been reconstructed. The translator of Irenaeus had a poor knowledge of Greek, or could not put Irenaeus' ideas into Latin; but he still had a great advantage over us—he had the original text before him, whereas all we have is a translation. We can at most find a Greek equivalent to a set of Latin words: we cannot be sure that these are exactly the words used by Irenaeus.

constituted."[38] This last remark must have had some special value to Irenaeus, we suppose; to us it is rather disconcerting. No doubt Irenaeus knew some things about the foundation of the Roman Church which we do not know today. In any case, if we take the Latin text as our starting-point, we cannot draw the conclusion that Irenaeus thought that the Church of Rome was founded and constituted by Peter and Paul simultaneously. There is a strong possibility that the Latin translator brought together, in his translation, two actions which were separate in the mind of Irenaeus—namely, the foundation and the constitution of the Church at Rome. "In it," he goes on, "the Apostolic Tradition was preserved by the succession of bishops." A little before, Irenaeus insists that anyone looking for the truth can find it in the Tradition of the Apostles, which every local church has preserved. So we must suppose he though that the Apostolic Tradition and the Faith proclaimed to mankind were preserved in the Roman Church more fully than in others, or, at least, in a more manifest way. Later, Irenaeus points to this Church—Rome—as the one to which all other churches must *convenire*. Nautin, like most of his predecessors, thinks the verb *convenire* means "to be in agreement or accord." But this is not the only possible meaning. I think a likelier sense of *convenire* here is "address oneself to," "turn to," "have recourse to." The sense of the remark would then be: every local church should have recourse to the Church of Rome. Irenaeus himself confirms this sense of *convenire* (*Adv. Haer.* III, 4, 1) in explaining what he had said about the Church of Rome:

> If at any time some simple question of detail should happen to provoke a dispute, surely the oldest churches, and those in which the Apostles lived, are the ones we should have recourse to (*recurrere*), and they will give us something very certain, and very clear, on the case in question.

This passage in Irenaeus illuminates the meaning of his remarks about the Church of Rome: if there are disputes in a local church, that church should have recourse to the Roman Church, for there is contained the Tradition which is preserved by all the churches.

The two meanings of *convenire*—accordance and recourse—are close but not identical. "Being in accord" would mean that the Church of Rome can declare the norms, like edicts, with regard to faith and church

38 P. Nautin, pp. 55–6.

discipline equally; and that the other churches must be in accord with these norms—in fact, they must accept them. This sense does not fit the context here, nor does it agree with what we know about the Church of Rome in the pre-Nicene period. The Church of Rome did not then initiate any decisions in the realm of faith, or of discipline either. Rome's vocation consisted in playing the part of arbiter, settling contentious issues by witnessing to the truth or falsity of whatever doctrine was put before them. Rome was truly the center where all converged if they wanted their doctrine to be accepted by the conscience of the Church. They could not count upon success except on one condition—that the Church of Rome had received their doctrine—and refusal from Rome predetermined the attitude the other churches would adopt. There are numerous cases of this recourse to Rome, but I will cite only one. According to Tertullian's story, Praxeas had managed to sway Pope Victor (or Zephyrinus) to condemn Montanism, and had also predisposed him, to some extent, in favor of monarchianism. In the treatise *Against Praxeas*, Tertullian's negative feelings toward Rome are plain to the reader; he says that Praxeas has crucified the Father and driven away the Paraclete. Praxeas obviously cannot have done this all by himself, and Tertullian's object of attack was not him, but the Church of Rome, which is accused of doing it for him. The Montanist Tertullian expresses the utmost dislike for "the great church," but he also understood very well that Rome's place and value were to be reckoned with: in his own words, Rome was the church *unde nobis quoque auctoritas praesta est.* This does not mean that the Church of Rome never settled any internal dogmatic question on its own initiative, as other Churches did; but generally the Roman bishops in this period preferred not to be involved in the dogmatic disputes going on at Rome. When they did interfere, the results were often unfortunate.

Let us return to the text of Irenaeus. He says that every local church, if contentious problems arise, must (*necesse*) have recourse to the Church of Rome. *Necesse* in Irenaeus does not suggest any legal obligation. The necessity springs from a more inward duty, reflecting the very nature of the Church: the duty of appealing, if there is disagreement, to the church which has the greatest authority. This church bore her witness on events in the other churches; or perhaps it would be more accurate to say, events in the Church. The witness was not a verdict backed by the force of law, and, as such, constraining the other churches to obey. It was a free act when the local churches followed Rome's witness; they were accepting witness from a fellow-church because of its higher authority. But Rome's witness was not less valid, but had higher validity than any and every legal verdict. If there has ever been a time in church history when the catch-word, *Roma locuta, causa finita*, stood for something real, that time was before the Church of Rome had any powers by law.

As Irenaeus saw things, the necessity of appealing to the Church of Rome was based on its *potentior principalitas*. What does this expression mean? Perhaps one day the relevant line from Irenaeus will be discovered in a Greek text; that would be the only chance of finding an answer to our question, an answer acceptable to all.[39] We have not yet been fortunate enough to find it, so we must be content with hypotheses for the present. There has been some progress recently made in interpreting Irenaeus' phraseology. Fewer and fewer defenders can be found for the view that Irenaeus means, by *potentior principalitas*, "primacy" of the Church of Rome, in the present-day sense. We should note that F. Sagnard, in his translation of the Third Book of *Adv. Haer.*, renders "*propter potentiorem principalitatem*" as "by reason of the more powerful authority of its foundation." This may not be altogether exact, but to me he seems correct in thinking that Irenaeus was talking about authority rather than power. But since, in the first place, we have no hope of finding the meaning of Irenaeus' word by the method of philological analysis, and in the second place, we cannot find the exact Greek equivalent, the problem seems to me soluble only if we start from Irenaeus' characteristic ideas. He was wont to say, "The Church of Rome is the very great, very ancient church, known to all others, and founded and constituted by Peter and by Paul." Might not *potentior principalitas* be simply an expression to describe Rome's particular position thus conceived? This church possesses the greatest authority among the churches; consequently it is the church with the priority. Surely, then, we could rightly say that the phrase *potentior principalitas* means "priority"; this would correspond with the Greek ἀρχαιότης. The fact that

39 See the analysis of the different meanings of *potentior principalitas* in F. Sagnard's *Irénée de Lyon, contre les Hérèses*, pp. 414ff.

this is the *greatest* priority shows that it is not the only one, and therefore does not exclude the priority of other churches in the more limited circles of local churches. Irenaeus had said himself, as we know, that litigious questions might be referred to churches founded by apostles, such as those of Smyrna and Ephesus.

The language of Irenaeus, thus interpreted, excludes the idea of Roman primacy. Dom B. Botte has rightly pointed out that Irenaeus was not the man who formulated primacy.[40] One might say, however, that he was the formulator of Roman priority among all local churches whatsoever. The tone of Irenaeus echoes Ignatius when he describes the particular position in which Rome stood, and which no other church shared. "Presiding in love" in Ignatius corresponds with the *potentior principalitas* in Irenaeus. Irenaeus also agrees with Ignatius in his recognition that certain churches have their own priority, in the more limited circles of local churches. Irenaeus, like Ignatius, bears witness to the attitude of local churches concerning the Church of Rome, and we can be quite sure that their witness was identical to the way the Roman Church itself viewed its own position. Thus, to Clement, on the one hand, and Ignatius and Irenaeus on the other, the priority enjoyed by the Roman Church was due to authority of witness: or, to use more modern language, it possessed priority of *receptio*. The Church of Rome had a special position, and this was not only the result of its actual status in fact; it also implied having a very definite ecclesiological system, which said that each local church was the Church of God in all its fullness. This system is what I have called eucharistic ecclesiology. Having made this analysis, I find one question still to be answered: to what extent did the Church of Rome, and particularly its bishops, act in accordance with their position, as I have explained it above?

7. I have already mentioned Clement of Rome and his way of understanding the position of the Church of Rome. Clement was obviously a man of mark, and his epistle to the Corinthians is an extremely important document; but his action still fails to supply an answer to the question we raised above. In his time, the Church of Rome had only recently taken cognizance of its prioritarian position. I lack the space

40 Dom B. Botte, "A propos de *l'Adversus Haereses* III, 3, 2, de saint Irénée," *Irenikon* XXX (1957/2) 162.

here to give an account of the history of the Roman Church in the pre-Nicene period; nor is it, indeed, called for. We know too little about some of the Roman bishops of that time; we cannot form an idea of how they regarded the position of the Roman Church; so I will be content to sketch the characters of two of these men, who are its most striking representatives—Pope Victor (189-198) and Pope Stephen (254–257).

Pope Victor, like Pope Stephen, has his place among the greatest men of action in the Roman Church. Some say, or rather insist, that Victor was the first Pope of Rome. This question—was Victor the first pope or not—is a matter for much discussion; but one thing is beyond doubt, that Victor, like Stephen, was an extremely colorful personality, a most commanding figure. Nobody in the pre-Nicene period acted like these two; but does this justify the conclusion that they understood the position of Rome in a way different from Irenaeus? Their own characters might suffice to make them act as they did, while yet remaining within the ancient ideological framework of priority. They were not alone in acting energetically. Did Cyprian act with less energy than Stephen? John Chrysostom and Basil the Great also showed great energy in action, yet nobody is going to say that they were the first popes of the Orient. Why then should we take Victor's energetic action as grounds for thinking him the first Pope of Rome?

When people speak of Victor as the first Pope, they have in mind his action during the Paschal controversies. In these controversies, many things still remain obscured from our sight. We do not really know why Victor raised the Paschal question; did it arise from a domestic situation inside the Roman Church, or was it first raised by the churches of Asia Minor? Eusebius (our only source) did not pass Victor's epistle down to us, which is strange, considering that he included the epistle of Polycrates in his *History*. We must not forget that when Victor addressed the churches of Asia Minor with a peremptory demand (if it was), he did so at a time when he had the backing of a virtual majority of churches. This peremptory demand surely means just that the Church of Rome had refused to accept the practice of Asia Minor. The churches of Asia Minor stood in isolation, since nearly all the other local churches had followed Victor's lead. Let us avoid the common mistake of talking about the churches of Asia Minor being "excommunicated." At the end of the second century, nobody thought it possible for one church to excommunicate another; nothing could be at issue beyond a breaking of brotherly communion between the churches. In his epistle to Victor, Irenaeus blames him for refusing to act in the gentle way of the presbyters, his predecessors; he did not accuse Victor of grasping special *power* over the Church for himself. Victor's behavior was still within the bounds of ordinary ecclesiastical practice. If Victor had ventured to go further than any one before him, the fact is easily explained by his character. Apparently he was of African origin; and in Carthage at this period there was a sort of Christian cult of Rome. We have only to recall the dithyrambic praise of Rome which we find in Tertullian's *De praescriptione haereticorum.* We simply have no data to justify the assertion that Victor, assuming the concept of the Universal Church, took the situation of the Roman Church to mean primacy of power.

As for Pope Stephen—has history treated him quite fairly? We nearly all start with a preconceived idea that, in the battle between him and Cyprian, Cyprian was right, and "the tyrant" (as Cyprian had called Stephen) was wrong. Did Stephen base his actions on a new ecclesiastical ideology, and did Cyprian keep to tradition? It would be more exact to say that neither of them kept to the traditional idea altogether, and that Cyprian had less respect for it than Stephen. Cyprian was possibly right in the case of the Spanish bishops, Basilides and Martial, but Stephen's behavior was perfectly in keeping with the prioritarian role which the Roman Church had to play. The principle of priority needed no modification to allow for his granting the pleas of the Spanish bishops. In Clement's time, the Corinthian presbyters had appealed to Rome with the same purpose, that is, to ask that no act of *receptio* should be made concerning the recent events in Corinth. Any church and any church member could appeal (*convenire* was Irenaeus' word) to any other church, and particularly to the church-in-priority. Cyprian asserts that the Spanish bishops were reinstated by Stephen.[41] But here we surely have something more like Cyprian's own interpretation. Stephen had refused to recognize the eviction of the Spanish bishops, and consequently the setting-up of new bishops in their place was also not countenanced. In other words, there was no *receptio* for this act. Stephen's

41 *Epist.* LXVII, V, 3.

behavior was perfectly natural, and in this case especially because Spain was in the direct sphere of Roman influence, not of Carthaginian. The Spanish churches, according to Cyprian, appealed to Carthage (that is, to the Carthaginian council of bishops) for comfort and help. The Carthaginian Church could have taken its own line and kept Rome informed, pointing out that Basilides had led Stephen into error. Cyprian did nothing of the sort. The Council, of which he was president, decided that the new bishops had been regularly established, and that their establishment could not be made invalid because their predecessors were improperly reestablished by Stephen. Even if Stephen's actions went beyond the limited scope which the Roman Church's priority allowed him—if, that is, he really did make the decision to reestablish the evicted bishops—Cyprian's action was nonetheless an innovation. He opposed the witness of the church-in-priority by the decisions of his council, and claimed for the council's decrees the force of law.

We will turn next to the baptismal controversies. I admit the great difficulty of forming an objective opinion about the actions of the two antagonists. Stephen's epistle has reached us through the comments made on it by Cyprian and Firmilian of Caesarea, both his enemies. Do their epistles give us the content of Stephen's epistle in a fair and exact way? It should be noted that the Latin text of Firmilian's epistle, found in the epistles of Cyprian, is not really a translation, but an adaptation from Firmilian's Greek original text: Cyprian wanted propaganda against Rome and adapted the text to suit his own angle.[42] This is why we cannot base our theories entirely on Firmilian's epistle. One further note; the question about the baptism of heretics and schismatics was not raised by Stephen in the first place: Cyprian started it, having for years pressed all churches, including Rome, to accept the practice of Carthage in this matter. Cyprian, supported on this point by the Councils of Carthage, did indeed reserve the right to every bishop to act as he saw fit, on the one condition of answering for his actions before God; but in fact he allowed no objections to stand in his way. Cyprian saw it not as an administrative problem, but as the *regula catholica*. A refusal to follow Cyprian's principles would indeed have created enormous practical diffi-

42 See J. Ludwig, *Die Primatwörte Mt. XVI,* 18, 19, *in der altkirchlicher Exegese* (Neutestamentliche Abhandlungen XIX Band, 4 Heft) (Münster, 1952), pp. 33–4.

culties. Imagine the case of a heretic—especially a Novatianist—enrolled in the Church by Rome and then migrating to Carthage. How would Cyprian have acted? In his eyes such a person had not received baptism.

Stephen flatly refused to follow Cyprian concerning the baptism of heretics. Is his refusal evidence that Stephen believed Rome's situation, and his own, to depend upon the notion of primacy and power? Why indeed *should* Stephen have followed Cyprian's line about the baptism of heretics when the Church of Rome had a different practice from that which Cyprian commended? Cyprian's extraordinary insistence shows that he, and not Stephen, was trying to exercise some sort of leadership over the whole Church by means of his councils. Stephen was probably first in citing the *logion* in Mt 16:18. But Cyprian drove him to do so. Had not Cyprian first sent to Rome his treatise *De Unitate Ecclesiae*, which uses the magic words *cathedra Petri*? Had he not written that whoever deserts "Peter's Chair" is putting himself outside the Church automatically? Had he not told Cornelius in his letter that Rome was *cathedra Petri et ecclesia principalis unde unitas sacerdotalis exorta est*?[43] If Stephen wrote, as Cyprian alleges, that he was the successor of Peter, such an assertion would not have gone beyond what Cyprian had said already. We must admit that Stephen's position was very difficult. First, Cyprian had rebelled against Stephen's decision when Stephen refused to recognize the deposition of the Spanish bishops. Next comes a peremptory demand that Stephen depose Marcian, the Bishop of Arles. It is no exaggeration to say that Cyprian wished Stephen to follow his directions, as his predecessor Cornelius had done before. But when Stephen took to speaking in Cyprian's style, Cyprian then found his own opinions inadmissible in Stephen's mouth; he rebelled against them passionately and brought against Stephen the councils he had convoked.

Of course Stephen's own mind may well have glided from one idea to another, and he may sometimes have taken the priority of the Roman Church to imply primacy of power. There is a world of difference between priority of authority, in the realm of witness, and primacy of power; but a change from the former to the latter was quite easy, once the idea of the Universal Church began to find favor. It came to Rome from various directions: from Carthage first of all. It next entered into

43 *Epist.* LIX, 14.

the religious mind through Jewish-Christian literature; and finally it found expression in Montanism. Apart from Gnostic literature, the *Didache* is the first document which contains any notion of the Universal Church; and in Montanism the idea of the Universal Church was actually put into practice. Before Catholic Rome had even come on the scene, claiming dominion over the Universal Church, there was a Montanist Rome at Pepuza.

Even supposing that Stephen wanted to be a real pope—and I think it unlikely—his was an isolated example and had no immediate consequences. Cyprian's ecclesiological system met opposition, even in his lifetime, and similar ill-success attended Stephen's attempts to carry out Cyprian's theory in practice, always supposing that he ever attempted anything of the sort. The doctrine of the Universal Church was not entirely accepted by the conscience of the pre-Nicene Period. Before the beginning of the Nicene period, Rome did not hold the primacy of power. After Stephen, the Roman Church forgot about "the Chair of Peter" for a long time. Is it not remarkable that the edicts of Gallienus, Licinius and Constantine seem unaware of the Universal Church and Rome its president? They only speak of local churches in isolation. Catholic theologians complain, with reason, that Constantine overshadowed the Bishop of Rome, and that Sylvester's pontificate was extremely insignificant.[44] To Constantine, the primacy of the Church of Rome did not exist. Further, it could not exist in his consciousness, because it had no legal character. And while it is true that the witness of pagan emperors and of the semi-Christian Constantine has no decisive value for us, it is hardly likely that when these emperors published their edicts of toleration, they could be unfamiliar with ecclesiastical organization. The decision of the Emperor Aurelian, in the case of Paul of Samosata, cannot be taken as evidence to support the primacy of the Bishop of Rome; the Emperor wanted evidence that Antioch was loyal, and saw a guarantee of this if the Bishop of Antioch were given recognition by his Italian colleagues and by the Bishop of Rome.

Now I only have one task left—to draw some conclusions from what I have been saying above. Universal ecclesiology, so prevalent in modern

44   A. Fliché and V. Martin, *Histoire de l'Église*, v. III (Paris, 1950), p. 36.

theology, is not really primitive. It came to replace eucharistic ecclesiology, which was the only one known in apostolic days. The foundations of universal ecclesiology were formulated for the first time by Cyprian of Carthage. With Constantine, a new factor comes into the Church's life, namely the Roman Empire and the Roman Caesar. This new factor led to the predominance of universal ecclesiology in the mind of the Church. In spite of all the difference there is between these two types of ecclesiology, they agree in both accepting the idea that the whole Church must follow a single directive. For the pattern of universal ecclesiology, a unique, personal power founded on rights is a necessity. It is impossible to construct a universal ecclesiology without admitting the idea of primacy, nothing but the exigencies of controversy could produce anything so artificial. The question of whether the primacy should belong to the Bishop of Rome or not is quite a different matter. In the pattern of eucharistic theology, power of one single bishop simply does not exist in any case, because power based on right does not exist. But this is not to say that eucharistic ecclesiology rejects the idea that the whole church should follow a single directive; this idea springs from the basic doctrine of eucharistic ecclesiology. According to this doctrine, one of the local churches possesses the priority, which is manifested in its greater authority of witness about events in other churches, that is, events in the Church of God in Christ, since every local church is the Church of God in Christ with all fullness. To put it otherwise, universal ecclesiology and eucharistic ecclesiology have different conceptions on the question of Church government: the first conceives this government as a matter of law and rights, and the second regards it as founded on grace. The idea of primacy, inherent in universal ecclesiology, is an idea subsequent to that of priority, just as this ecclesiology was subsequent to eucharistic ecclesiology; the concept of primacy is really the same as that of priority, only looked at from a lawyer's point of view. This explains why, in the pattern of universal ecclesiology, the primacy belongs to one of the bishops, who is at the head of the Universal Church; but in the pattern of eucharistic ecclesiology, the priority belongs to one of the local churches, and only belongs to the bishop through his church. No priority belongs to the bishop personally; he possesses it only through the local church. Priority is a concept founded on the idea of grace: it is a gift of grace, given by God to one of the local churches; and its nature is a gift of witnessing, in the name of the Church, about all that goes on within the same Church. This shows that everything happens *in* the Church, not outside it or *over* it. For this reason—that priority is a gift of witness—it cannot be fully accounted for on empirical grounds. We cannot explain why the apostle Peter occupied a special place among the apostles and had a special mission, nor why Paul was chosen by God to be the apostle to the Gentiles, nor yet why the priority, first possessed by the Church of Jerusalem, was handed on to Rome. The end of the reckoning brings us to a dilemma: we have simply to accept either priority and eucharistic ecclesiology or primacy and universal ecclesiology. By denying both we reject the idea that the Church has a single directive—and that is an essential proposition in the doctrine of the Church.

The Orthodox Church is absolutely right in refusing to recognize the contemporary doctrine that primacy belongs to the Bishop of Rome; however, this rightness does not lie in the numerous arguments that have been brought against primacy, but in the very fact of non-recognition. The arguments against primacy offered by Orthodox school-theology seem to suffer from some lack of clarity and finish. This can be explained by the fact that eucharistic ecclesiology is still alive, deep down, in the Orthodox soul; but Orthodoxy on the surface is under the shadow of universal ecclesiology, and also of contemporary ecclesiastical organization. The attribute of "catholicity," which (in eucharistic ecclesiology) belongs to the episcopal church, has now been transferred to the auto-cephalous church—a unit, in fact, half political and half ecclesiastical. Naturally, the episcopal church loses its catholicity and becomes a part of the autocephalous church. To this latter, alone, modern Orthodox theology ascribes the ability to be free and autonomous. Orthodox theology indeed rejects the idea of primacy on the universal scale, but it recognizes a partial primacy at the center of every autocephalous church, a primacy belonging to the head of that church. We are concerned here with primacy, not priority, for priority implies that every local church has fullness of ecclesiastical *esse*. The autocephalous churches, meanwhile, have become divided and separated, for the idea of a single directive has faded since the fall of Byzantium. Ever since the second Ecumenical

Council, Constantionple has been trying to bring off a pan-Orthodox primacy, but all her attempts have failed. It would be most unwise to talk of an "Eastern Pope," as though the Patriarch of Constantinople set himself to copy the Bishop of Rome, and wrong whether we take an ideological or a historical view. But no doubt various inner motives did impel the Patriarch of Constantinople to follow along the road to primacy, within the pattern of a universal ecclesiology. In modern times, the unity of the Orthodox Church is becoming a sort of abstract ideal, with no means of manifesting itself in the real life of the Church. Anyone who regards the pan-Orthodox or Ecumenical Council as an organ manifesting the Church's unity is just putting things in the wrong order, consequences before foundation. In fact, the pan-Orthodox Council should be the consequence of Orthodox Church unity; it should be guided by a church or a bishop; and it cannot be a foundation for this unity.

In the long course of the struggle against the Roman Catholic position about the primacy of Rome, Orthodox doctrine has lost the very notion of priority. And the Catholic Church lost sight of the idea even earlier, during its struggle for a single directive in the Church, which it has now transformed into primacy. If we take the respective positions of the two churches as they stand, there is no hope of resolving the question of primacy. We can only accept the tragedy, but with our eyes open, and without that romantic sentimentality which only adds bitterness to the everlasting discussion about primacy. "The unity of the faith in the bond of peace." Unity of faith still reigns within the Orthodox Church, but without union in love; and neither exists between the Orthodox and the Roman Catholic Churches. Why is this? Surely because the mind of the Church has become unaware that the Church of God should be directed by a local church, one church among all the others. They all possess catholicity; but priority of authority, by giving witness about events in the Church's life, is something that belongs only to the church "which presides in love."

5

The Idea Of Primacy In Orthodox Ecclesiology

Alexander Schmemann

I

By primacy we mean here an ecclesiastical power, superior to that of a bishop, whose jurisdiction is limited to his diocese. In Church history and canonical tradition we find the following forms of primacy:

(1) regional primacy—within an ecclesiastical province or metropolitan district, i.e., in a group of dioceses (as defined, for example, in Apostolic Canon 33);

(2) primacy within the so-called *autocephalous churches*: the power of a patriarch or archbishop (e.g.,the Patriarch of Moscow); and

(3) *universal primacy*: that of Rome or Constantinople.[1]

But if facts are known, their ecclesiological interpretation is virtually absent from Orthodox theology. We badly need a clarification of the nature and functions of all these primacies and, first of all, of the very concept of primacy. For both in theory and in practice there is a great deal of confusion concerning the definition of the "supreme power" in the church, of its scope and modes of expression. Of the three types of primacy mentioned above, only the second—the primacy within the autocephalous church, is defined more or less precisely in each particular "autocephaly." But even here the ecclesiological dimension is obviously lacking and the great variety of existing patterns—from the almost absolute "monarchy" of the Russian Patriarch to the more or less nominal primacy of the Archbishop of Athens—reveals the absence of a common understanding of primacy, or of a consistent canonical theory

---

1 For the description and canonical analysis of various forms of primacy, cf N. Zaozerskii, *Ecclesiastical Power* (Sergiev Posad, 1894, in Russian), pp. 218ff.

of it. For two hundred years, Russian bishops and canonists denounced the synodal government instituted by Peter the Great as uncanonical, yet it was recognized as canonical by the other Eastern churches.[2] Why is the present patriarchal monarchy in Russia (the bishops even call the Patriarch their "father") more canonical than the collective government or the Holy Synod? What are, in other terms, the criteria of canonicity? Obviously no existing administrative system can simply be equated with canonical tradition. In the empirical life of the Church one administrative system is replaced by another, and each of them is the result of a "canonical adjustment," i.e., the application of the canonical tradition to a particular situation. Yet only a clear understanding of the canonical tradition itself, with all of its theological and ecclesiological implications, can supply us with solid criteria for a canonical evaluation of any such "adjustment" and for measuring its *canonicity*.[3]

As to the *regional* and *universal* types of primacy, there does not exist even a *de facto* consensus of Orthodox opinion. Regional primacy, although it is clearly sanctioned by our canonical tradition,[4] has practically disappeared from the structure and the life of the Orthodox Churches in the triumph of centralized autocephalies. And the idea of universal primacy is either rejected as alien to the very spirit of Orthodoxy or formulated in terms so vague and ambiguous that, instead of solving, they only obscure the whole of primacy.[5]

And yet the solution of this problem is certainly on the agenda for our time. It would not be difficult to prove that the canonical and jurisdictional troubles and divisions, of which we have had too many in the last

2   Much pertaining material has been gathered in the *Opinions* of Russian bishops, presented for the Pre-Sobor Convocation of 1906–12.
3   Cf. N. Afanassieff, "The Canons of the Church: Changeable or Unchangeable?" *St Vladimir's Theological Quarterly* 11 (1967) no. 2, pp. 54-68; and also his article "The Canons and the Canonical Consciousness" in *Put'* (1933) (in Russian).
4   F. Zaozerskii, pp. 228ff.—P. V. Gidulianov, *The Metropolitan in the First Three Centuries* (Moscow, 1905, in Russian)—N. Milash, *The Canons of the Orthodox Church, with Commentaries* (St Petersburg, 1911, in Russian), vol. 1, pp. 70ff.—Th. Balsamon in Rhallis-Potlis, *Syntagma*, 2, 171—V. Bolotov, *Lectures in the History of Ancient Church* (St Petersburg, 1913, in Russian), Vol. 3, pp. 210ff.—V. Myshtsyn, *The Organization of the Church in the First Two Centuries* (St Petersburg, 1909).
5   Cf. for example, the controversy aroused by the Encyclical Letter of the Ecumenical Patriarch for the Sunday of Orthodoxy in 1950; details and bibliography in my article, "The Ecumenical Patriarch and the Orthodox Church," in *Tserkovnyi Vestnik*, Paris, 1951.

decades, have their roots in some way or other in this question of primacy or, to be more exact, in the absence of a clearly defined doctrine of the nature and functions of primacy. And the same unsolved problem constitutes a major handicap for the unity and, therefore, the progress of Orthodoxy in countries like America, where, paradoxically enough, the loyalty to a certain concept of "canonicity" leads to the most uncanonical situation that can be imagined: the coexistence on the same territory of a number of parallel "jurisdictions" and dioceses...[6] Finally, there can be little doubt that ecclesiology, the doctrine of the Church, is today at the very center of our relations with the non-Orthodox. Among Roman Catholic theologians, there is a growing interest, and not only a "polemical" one, in Orthodox views on primacy; as to the Protestants, it is of vital importance that they understand our concept of the Church's universality. There are thus reasons for a genuinely theological reconsideration of the whole question. And even if no final answer can be given immediately, it will not be reached without a sustained theological effort.

II

We have defined *primacy* as a form of power. This definition, however, must be qualified at once. For there is a preliminary question: is there in Orthodoxy a power superior to that of a bishop, i.e., the power *over* the bishop, and hence over the Church of which he is the head? This question is essential for the whole problem of primacy.[7] But the answers given it by ecclesiology on the one hand, and the various ecclesiastical administrative systems on the other hand, are contradictory. Theologically and ecclesiologically the answer should be "no": there can be no power *over* the bishop and his Church (i.e., diocese) for, "if power

6   Thus it is obvious, for example, that the fatal "jurisdictional" divisions in the Russian Church outside Russia are ultimately rooted in the question of ecclesiastical *submission* to the various "supreme authorities," i.e., in the problem of primacy. Cf. my essays *The Church and the Ecclesiastical Structure* (Paris, 1949, in Russian)—"A Controversy on the Church," in *Tserkovnyi Vestnik* (1953), 2—"On Neo-Papism," *ibid.* (1951) (all in Russian). The development of church life in America, on the other hand, is deeply handicapped by the absence of any connections between the ten Orthodox national jurisdictions, which for the lack of a *center of communion* are practically isolated from each other. Here also the problem of primacy, and consequently of an *initiative* toward a "rapprochement," is quite central.

7   N. Afanassieff, *The Lord's Table* (Paris, 1955, in Russian)—*The Office of the Laity in the Church* (Paris, 1955, in Russian).

belongs to the Church as one of its constituent elements, it must correspond to the nature of the Church and not be heterogeneous to it."[8] The ministry of power and government, as all other ministries within the Church, is a *charism*, a gift of grace. It is bestowed through the sacrament of order, for only sacramentally received power is possible in the Church, whose very nature is grace and whose very *institution* is based on grace. And the Church has only three charismatic orders, with no gift of power superior to that of a bishop. No sacramental order of primacy, no charism of primacy exists, therefore, in the Orthodox Church; if it existed it would have a nature different from grace and, consequently, its source would not be the Church.

But in the present canonical structure of the Church such *supreme power* not only exists, but is commonly understood as the foundation of the Church, and the basis of its canonical system.[9] Theoretically, it is true, a personal power of one bishop over another bishop is rejected; the "supreme power" is exercised usually by the primate together with the governing body: synod, council, etc....For us, however, the important fact is that such supreme ecclesiastical government is always characterized as power over bishops, who are therefore subordinated to it. "Supreme power" is thus introduced into the very structure of the Church as its essential element. The divorce between canonical tradition and the canonical facts is nowhere more obvious than in this universal triumph of the notion of supreme power. Having rejected and still rejecting it in its Roman form, i.e., as universal power, the Orthodox conscience has easily accepted it in the so-called "autocephalies."

In this situation the question we have formulated above cannot be answered simply by references to historical precedent or canonical texts, isolated from their context, as it is too often done in contemporary canonical controversies. We must go deeper into the very sources of Orthodox doctrine of the church, to the essential laws of her organization and life.

---

8 N. Afanassieff, "The Power of Love," in *Tserkovnyi Vestnik* 22 (1950/1) 4 (in Russian).
9 Cf. for example, the Statutes of the Russian Church as adopted by the Council of 1917–18—"in the Orthodox Church in Russia the *Supreme Power* belongs to the Local Council..." "The Diocese is a part of the Russian Church."

III

Orthodox tradition is unanimous in its affirmation of the Church as an organic unity. This organism is the Body of Christ and the definition is not merely symbolic, but expresses the very nature of the Church.[10] It means that the visible organizational structure of the Church is the manifestation and realization of the Body of Christ, or in other terms, that this structure is rooted in the Church as the Body of Christ. But one must stress immediately that if the doctrine of the Church-Body of Christ is both scriptural and traditional, it has never really been elaborated and interpreted theologically. For reasons which cannot be discussed here (we shall mention some of them later), this doctrine disappeared rather early from canonical (i.e., ecclesiological) thinking both in the West and East, and its neglect by canonists constitutes, no doubt, a tragedy the results of which mark all domains of ecclesiastical life and thought. In the early church, the canonical tradition was an integral part of ecclesiology—of the living *experience* of the Church. But little by little it became an autonomous sphere in which the visible ecclesiastical structures, the functions of power and authority, and the relations between Churches, ceased to be explained in terms of the Church-Body of Christ. Loosing its ties with ecclesiology, the canonical tradition became "canon law." But in canon law there was no room for the notion of the Body of Christ, because this notion has nothing to do with "law." The life of the Church came to be expressed in juridical terms, and the canons which originally were (and essentially still are) an ecclesiological testimony were transformed into, and used as, juridical norms.[11] The "mystery of the

---

10 Among Russian theologians F. E. Akvilonov, *The Church: The Doctrinal definitions of the Church and the Apostolic doctrine of the Church as the Body of Christ* (St Petersburg, 1894, in Russian)—V. Troitskii, *Essays in the History of the Doctrine of the Church* (Sergiev Posad, 1912, in Russian)—G. Florovsky, "L'Eglise, sa nature et sa tache," in *L'Eglise Universelle dans le dessein de Dieu* (Paris, 1948). On biblical and patristic ecclesiology cf. P. Mersch, *Le Corps Mystique du Christ, Etudes de Théologie Historique* (2 vols., Paris, 1933–6)—G. Bardy, *La Théologie de l'Eglise suivant S. Paul* (Paris, 1943)—*La Théologie de l'Eglise de S. Clément de Rome à S. Irénée* (Paris, 1945)—*La Théologie de l'Eglise de S. Irénée au Concile de Nicée* (Paris, 1947)—L. Bouyer, *L'Incarnation et l'Eglise Corps du Christ dans la théologie de S. Athanase* (Paris, 1943)—H. du Manoir, "L'Eglise Corps du Christ, chez Cyrille d'Alexandrie," in *Dogme et Spiritualité chez S. Cyrille d'A.* (Paris, 1944), pp. 287–366, cf. also S. Jaki, *op. cit*, pp. 154–203.

11 We find in Suvorov, *Canon Law* (Iaroslavl, 1889, in Russian), Vol. I, p. 5, a classical expression of this juridical understanding of the Church—"The Church, being a visible society, cannot be outside *law*...As a society, it consists of several members, linked to each other by certain relations that grow out of their life in the Church, and it also has an

Church" was neither denied nor forgotten. It simply ceased to be under-stood as the only *law* of the whole life of the Church.[12]

Today, however, an ecclesiological revival is taking place. And it is moved primarily by the desire to *express* the Church—her life, her structures, her visible unity—in adequate theological terms, and first of all in terms of the Body of Christ. It is within this revival and in connection with this "rediscovery" of the traditional concept of the Body that new attempts are made to clarify the basic ecclesiological notions of *organism* and *organic unity*. And these, in turn, shape and condition the whole understanding of *primacy*.

The Church is an *organism*. The Church is *organic unity*. In a series of articles the contemporary Russian theologian and canonist, Fr N. Afanassieff, shows that there existed (and still exist) two ecclesiological "elaborations" or interpretations of this organic unity: the *universal* and the *eucharistic*.[13] This distinction, we shall see, is of capital importance for the understanding of the Orthodox idea of primacy.[14]

Universal ecclesiology finds its fullest expression in Roman Catholic theology, crowned by the Vatican dogma of 1870. Here the only ade-quate expression of the Church as organism is the universal structure of the Church, its universal unity. The Church is the *sum* of all local churches, which all together *constitute* the Body of Christ. The Church is thus conceived in terms of *whole* and *parts*. Each community, each local church is but a part, a member of this universal organism; and it participates in the Church only through its belonging to the "whole." In the words of one of its best exponents, Roman theology seeks a definition of the Church in which "*parts* would receive within the whole, conceived really as a whole, the status of genuine *parts*."[15]

organization with a particular sphere of activity for each organ...The regulation of relations, spheres of activities, and all the ways and means leading to the fulfillment of the Church's purpose require the *order of law.*" And since "the ways and means" imply practically all aspects of Church life, this means that the whole life of the Church requires the order of law. Outside this order there remains only the Church as "object of faith" (*ibid.*, p. 6).

12   This lack of ecclesiology in theological development has recently been stressed by G. Florovsky, and J. Congar in his *Vraie et Fausse Réforme dans l'Eglise.*
13   N. Afanassieff, "Two Ideas of Church Universal" in *Put'* (1933) 16.
14   N. Afanasieff, "The Catholic Church" in *Pravoslavnaia Mysl'* 11 (1957) 17-44.
15   J. Congar, *Chrétiens Désunis* (Paris, 1937), p. 241; cf. also my essay "Unity, Division, Reunion in the Light of Orthodox Ecclesiology," in *Theologia* (Athens, 1951).

We do not need to go here into all details of this ecclesiology. The important point here is for us to see that in the light of this doctrine the need for and the reality of a universal head, i.e., the Bishop of Rome, can no longer be termed an exaggeration. It becomes not only acceptable but necessary. If the Church is a universal organism, she must have at her head a universal bishop as the focus of her unity and the organ of supreme power. The idea, popular in Orthodox apologetics, that the Church can have no visible head, because Christ is her *invisible* head, is theological nonsense.[16] If applied consistently, it should also eliminate the necessity for the visible head of each local church, i.e., the bishop. Yet it is the basic assumption of a "catholic" ecclesiology that the visible structure of the Church manifests and communicates its invisible nature. The invisible Christ is made present through the visible unity of the bishop and the people: the Head and the Body.[17] To oppose the *visible* structure to the *invisible* Christ leads inescapably to the Protestant divorce between a visible and human Church which is contingent, relative and changing, and an invisible Church in heaven. We must simply admit that if the categories of organism and organic unity are to be applied primarily to the Church universal as the sum of all its component parts (i.e., local churches), then the one, supreme, and universal power as well as its bearer becomes a self-evident necessity, because this unique visible organism must have a unique visible head. Thus the efforts of Roman Catholic theologians to justify Roman primacy not by mere historical contingencies but by divine institution appear as logical. Within a universal ecclesiology, primacy is of necessity *power* and, by the same necessity, a divinely instituted power; we have all this in a consistent form in the Roman Catholic doctrine of the Church.

IV

Is this ecclesiology acceptable from the Orthodox point of view? The question may seem naive. The Orthodox Church has rejected as heretical

16 Here is an example from an article directed against the very idea of a universal center in the Church: "Not only has the Orthodox Church never had such a center, but this idea completely destroys the mystery of Orthodox ecclesiology, where the Risen Christ, invisibly present, is the center of the Church" (E. Kovalevsky, "Ecclesiological Problems—On the articles of Fr Sophrony and Fr A. Schmemann," in *Vestnik Zapadno-Evrop. Ekzarkhata* [Paris, 1950], 2–3, p. 14). This argument is far from being a new one...

17 Ignatius of Antioch, *Smyrn.* 8, 2.

the Roman claims and thus has implicitly condemned the ecclesiology which supports them. This answer, however, while correct in theory, is not the one which we find in fact, in the reality of life. We must remember that the rejection of Roman claims at the time of the Great Schism was due to an Orthodox "instinct" more than to a positive ecclesiological doctrine. It was helped by violent anti-Roman feelings among the Easterners, and by the whole alienation and estrangement of the West from the East. It is well-known today what atmosphere of hatred, mutual suspicion and bitterness accompanied the doctrinal controversies, adding an emotional dimension[18] to the dogmatical rupture. The rejection of Roman errors did not result in a positive elaboration of the Orthodox doctrine, as was the case after the condemnation of Arianism, Nestorianism, etc. Our ecclesiology is still lacking an "oros," similar to the Nicean Creed in Triadology or the Chalcedonian definition in Christology. But at the time of the schism, church conscience both in the West and in the East was deeply affected by ideas alien to Orthodox ecclesiology. We shall deal with some of them later. Here we must stress that all of them were a denial *de facto* of the living sources of the eucharistic *ecclesiology* which constitutes, in our opinion, the basis of the true canonical tradition. I say *de facto*, because the Orthodox Church, different in this respect from Rome, has never transformed this denial into a doctrine, into an ecclesiological system. Various types of "canon law" have neither poisoned the prime sources of Church life, nor abolished or replaced the canonical tradition. Thus there is the possibility of a return to them.

What then, from the point of view which interests us in this essay, is the essence of this Orthodox ecclesiology? It is, above all, that it applies the categories of *organism* and *organic unity* to "the Church of God abiding..." in every place: to the local church, to the community led by a bishop and having, in communion with him, the *fullness* of the Church. Fr Afanassieff terms it "eucharistic ecclesiology." And, indeed, it is rooted in the eucharist as the Sacrament of the Church, an act which ever realizes the Church as the *Body of Christ*.[19] A similar view is expressed by Fr George Florovsky. "The Sacraments," he writes, "consti-

18 Many details in my unpublished essay, "The Unionistic Problem in the Byzantine Church."
19 N. Afanassieff, in *Pravoslavnaia Mysl'* 11, pp. 21ff.

tute the Church. Only in them does the Christian community transcend its human dimensions and become the Church."[20] Through the eucharist, we have the whole Christ and not a "part" of Him; and therefore the Church which is "actualized" in the eucharist is not a "part" or "member" of a whole, but the Church of God in her wholeness. For it is precisely the function of the eucharist to manifest the whole Church, her "catholicity." Where there is the eucharist, there is the Church; and, conversely, only where the whole Church is (i.e., the people of God united in the bishop, the head, the shepherd), there is the eucharist. Such is the primitive ecclesiology expressed in the tradition of the early church and still recognizable in our canons and in the liturgical "rubrics," which to so many seem obscure and non-essential.[21] There is no room here for the categories of the "parts" and of the "whole," because it is the very essence of the sacramental hierarchical structure that in it a "part" not only "agrees" with, but is identical to, the whole, reveals it adequately in itself, and in one word *is* the whole. The local church as a sacramental organism, as the gift of God in Christ, is not part or member of a wider universal organism. She is the Church. Objectively, as the Body of Christ, the Church is always identical to herself in space and time. In time, because she is always the people of God gathered to proclaim the death of the Lord and to confess his resurrection. In space, because in each local church the fullness of gifts is given, the whole truth is announced, the whole Christ is present, who is "yesterday and today and forever the same." In her sacramental and hierarchical order, the Church reveals and conveys to men the fullness of Christ into which they must grow (cf. Eph 4:13).

The essential corollary of this "eucharistic" ecclesiology is that it excludes the idea of a *supreme power*, understood as power *over* the local church and her bishop. The ministry of power, as all ministries and

20 G. Florovsky, p. 65; N. Zaozerskii, pp. 21ff.
21 Limitations of space prevent me from dealing adequately with the connection between ecclesiology and liturgical theology; cf. my article "Liturgical Theology: its Task and Method" in *St Vladimir's Seminary Quarterly* 1 (1957/4) 16-27. There can be little doubt that all rubrics and rules concerning the unity of the eucharistic gathering (one eucharist a day on the same altar by the same celebrant, etc.) have an ecclesiological significance, i.e., they preserve the meaning of eucharist as an expression of the unity and fullness of the Church. Outside this ecclesiological significance they become meaningless, and as a matter of fact, are more and more frequently ignored or "by-passed" (second altar, "special liturgies," etc.).

charisms, has its source in and is performed within the organic unity of the Church. It is rooted in the sacraments, whose aim is to fulfill the Church as the Body of Christ. This ministry of power belongs to the bishop and there is no ministry of any higher power. A *supreme power* would mean power *over* Christ himself. The bishop is vested with power, yet the root of this power is in the Church, in the eucharistic gathering, at which he presides as priest, pastor and teacher. "Power" in the Church can be defined and understood only within the indivisible unity of the Church, the eucharist and the bishop. It cannot have a source different from that of the Church herself: the presence of Christ in the sacrament of the "new aeon," of the life in the Spirit. And for the early church all this was a living reality, such that it would not be difficult to show that this reality shaped the foundations of the canonical tradition.[22] When, for example, our present and highly "juridical" canon law affirms that all bishops are *equal in grace*, does this not mean what has been affirmed above? For what is the grace of the episcopate if not the "charism" of power? And since the Church knows of no other charism of power, there can exist no *power* higher than that of the bishop.[23]

V

Does all this mean that Orthodox ecclesiology simply rejects the very notion of *primacy*? No. But it rejects the fatal error of universal ecclesiology which identifies primacy with power, transforming the latter from a ministry in the Church into power over the Church. To explain the Orthodox conception of primacy, we must now consider the approach of eucharistic ecclesiology towards the Church universal. It must be stated

22 The basic fact for any theological interpretation of the power of the bishop (or priest) is the absolute connection between ordination and eucharist. This connection is usually viewed as self-evident, yet it constitutes the starting point for a "theology of power" as *power of grace*.

23 I cannot deal here with the difficult problem of the *parish* in its relation to the diocese. Evidently, the early church knew only the community headed by the bishop, who was the normal celebrant of the eucharist, the teacher and the pastor of his church. The presbyters constituted his council—the *presbyterium*—F. J. Colson, *L'Evêque dans les communautés primitives* (Paris, 1951)—H. Chirat, *L'Assemblée Chrétienne à l'âge apostolique* (Paris, 1949) and the symposium *Etudes sur le Sacrament de l'Ordre* (Paris, 1957). The division of the diocese into parishes and the corresponding transformation of the presbyter into a parish rector came later, and this change has never been seriously studied and interpreted theologically. In any case, it cannot contradict the basic principles of eucharistic ecclesiology, for it would then contradict the nature of the Church.

emphatically that this type of ecclesiology does not transform the local church into a self-sufficient monad, without any "organic" link with other similar monads. There is no "congregationalism" here.[24] The organic unity of the Church universal is not less real than the organic unity of the local church. But if universal ecclesiology interprets it in terms of "parts" and "whole," for eucharistic ecclesiology the adequate term is that of *identity*: "the Church of God abiding in..." The Church of God is the one and indivisible Body of Christ, wholly and indivisibly present in each church, i.e., in the visible unity of the people of God, the bishop and the eucharist. And if universal unity is indeed *unity of the church* and not merely *unity of churches*, its essence is not that all churches together constitute one vast, unique organism, but that each church—in the identity of order, faith and gifts of the Holy Spirit—is the *same* Church, the same Body of Christ, indivisibly present wherever is the "ecclesia." It is thus the same organic unity of the church herself, the "churches" being not complementary to each other, as parts or members, but each one and all of them together being nothing else, but the One, Holy, Catholic, and Apostolic Church.

It is this ontological identity of all churches with the Church of God that establishes the connecting link between churches, making them the Church universal. For the fullness (*pleroma*) of each local church not only does not contradict her need for other churches and, indeed, her *dependence* on them, but implies them as her own *conditio sine qua non*. On the one hand, the fullness of each local church is the same that is given to every other church; it is a fullness possessed in common as the gift of God. And on the other hand, she has it only in agreement with all other churches, and only inasmuch as she does not separate herself from this agreement, does not make the one and indivisible gift her own, "private" gift...

"A new bishop shall be installed by all bishops of the province...."

In this Canon 4 of the Council of Nicaea—which simply sanctions an already existing practice (cf. Hippolytus' *Apostolic Tradition*)—we find

24 Cf. the already mentioned articles of E. Kovalevsky and also Hierom. Sophrony, "The Unity of the Church in the Image of Trinity," in *Vestnik Zapadno-Evrop. Ekzarkhata* (Paris, 1950), 2–3, pp. 8–33.

the first and the most comprehensive form of the *interdependence* of several churches. The local church receives the condition and the "note" of her fullness—the episcopate—through the bishops of other churches. What is the meaning of this dependence? The universal—"whole-and-parts"—ecclesiology uses this canon as its main justification and proof: the plurality of the consecrators signifies the "whole" to which the local church—the "part"—is therefore subordinated.[25] Such an interpretation could appear only at a time when the real link between the bishop and his church was forgotten and the charism of episcopacy had come to be thought of as a personal gift which any "two or three" bishops could bestow on any one, and when "valid consecration" became the only content of the notion of apostolic succession. The meaning of this canon appears quite different if we look into the early practice of the Church as described, for example, in the *Apostolic Tradition* of Hippolytus. The consecration of a bishop is followed by the eucharist, which is offered by the newly consecrated bishop and not by any of the consecrators.[26] This seemingly minor "liturgical" detail expresses in fact an important norm of primitive ecclesiology. From the moment he is elected and consecrated, the bishop is the president of the eucharistic assembly, i.e., the head of the Church, and his consecration finds its fulfillment when for the first time he offers to God the eucharist of the church. Thus the consecration of a bishop is first of all the *testimony* that this man, elected by his own church, is elected and appointed by God, and that through his election and consecration his church is identical with the Church of God which abides in all churches...[27] It is not the transfer of a gift by those who possess it, but the manifestation of the fact that the *same* gift, which they have received in the Church from God, has now been given to this bishop in this church. Episcopate is not a "collective gift" which any "two or three" bishops can convey to another man, but a ministry in the Church, a gift given to the Church; therefore the *cheirotonia* of a bishop bears testimony that the Church *has* received it. The unbroken episcopal succession, which was the decisive argument in the polemics

---

25 N. Milash, pp. 46–7; cf. Dom. B. Botte, "L'Ordre d'après les prières d'ordination," in *Le Sacrament de l'ordre,* p. 31.

26 Hippolytus of Rome, *Apost. Tradition,* I, 4.

27 On the notion of *witness* in sacraments cf. N. Afanassieff, "Sacramenta et Sacramentalia," in *Pravoslavnaia Mysl'* 10.

against gnosticism, was understood primarily as the succession of bishops within every church and not in terms of "consecrators."[28] Today, however, the emphasis in the doctrine of apostolic succession has shifted to the question of consecrators. But such was not the meaning given this doctrine by St Irenaeus;[29] for in spite of the fact that no bishop could be consecrated by his predecessor in the same chair, it is precisely this succession in the chair which is all-important to St Irenaeus and is to him the proof of the "identity" of the Church in time and space with the Church of God, with the fullness of Christ's gift—for "the Church is in the bishop and the bishop is in the Church." The consecration of a bishop by other bishops is thus the acknowledgment of the will of God as being fulfilled in this particular church. This fulfillment includes, to be sure, the bestowing of the charism of the Holy Spirit upon the candidate, and from this point of view the consecrators are *the* ministers of the sacrament of order. But this they are because of their function and ministry in the Church and not in virtue of a power over grace, inherent to their "rank." Sacramental theology has dealt almost exclusively with the *right* of the bishops to consecrate other bishops, but it has badly neglected the ecclesiological *content* and meaning of this right, which comes precisely from the bishop's function as *witness* of God's will in the Church, his "charism" being to keep the Church in the will of God and guide her towards its fulfillment. The church whose bishop has died has also lost the power to express this testimony. The testimony, therefore, must of necessity come from other churches and through their ministers who have the charism of proclaiming the will of God. In other terms, this aspect of *testimony* (the absence of which may lead eventually to an almost magical understanding of the sacrament of order) is essential to the consecration; while the gift of the Spirit comes not *from* the bishops, yet their presence, unity and testimony are the signs of its having been given to this particular church by God himself; they are indeed the "form" of the sacrament.[30]

The dependence of each church on other churches is thus a depen-

---

28 J. Meyendorff in *Orthodoxy and Catholicity* (New York: Sheed and Ward, 1966), p. 6.

29 Cf. Iren. of Lyons, *Adv. Haer.* IV, III, 3, and G. Bardy, *La Théologie de l'Eglise de S. Clément de Rome à S. Irénée*, pp. 183ff. On *diadoche* in Irenaeus cf. E. Caspar, *Die älteste Römische Bischofliste* (Berlin, 1926), p. 444.

30 For this reason both *election* and *ordination* are essential and necessary elements in the Orthodox rite of the appointment of bishops.

dence not of submission but of testimony: each church testifying about all others and all together testifying about each that they are *one* in faith and life, and that separately and all together they are the Church of God—the indivisible gift of the new life in Christ. Each church has fullness in herself, acknowledged and fulfilled in the unity of the bishop and the people; and it is the identity of this fullness with the fullness of the Church of God (and, therefore, with the "pleroma" of every other church) that is both expressed and maintained in the consecration of a new bishop by other bishops. Thus the organic unity of the Church as Body of Christ does not divide her into "parts" nor make the life of any local church "partial"; it prevents the isolation of the local church into a self-sufficient organism with no need for other churches. And we should add that the conscience of the universal unity of the Church, of living *koinonia* and mutual responsibility and the joy of belonging to the one household of God, has never been stronger than during the short triumph of precisely this type of ecclesiology.[31]

VI

The sacrament of episcopal consecration reveals the first and the essential form of *primacy,* or rather the basis for primacy: the *synod of bishops.* In Orthodoxy, the synod is usually given an exceptional importance. The Church is often described as the "Church of the Councils," and her government as "conciliary" (*sobornyi* in Russian). But very little has been done to define the nature and function of synods in theological terms. Canonically, the synod is interpreted as the "supreme authority" in the Church. Such, we have seen, is the inescapable logic of canon law once it has ceased to be governed internally by the doctrine of the Church as Body of Christ. In fact, to the Roman doctrine of a *personal* supreme power one opposed, on the Orthodox side, the theory of a collective supreme power; and in contemporary controversies the only question debated is that of the limits of such a "college"—whether it should consist of bishops only or include "representatives" from both clergy and laity. This theory acquired a new vitality after it was combined—in a rather inconsistent way—with the slavophile teaching about "sobornost," and this combination made it possible with a clear con-

31 Iren. of Lyons, *Adv. Haer.* III, 24, I.

science to accuse Roman Catholicism of being overjuridical in its ecclesiology.

However, the idea of the synod as "the visible supreme constitutive and governing organ of church power"[32] corresponds neither to the slavophile doctrine of "sobornost"[33] nor to the original function of the synod in the Church. The synod is not "power" in the juridical sense of this word, for there can exist no power over the Church Body of Christ. The synod is, rather, a *witness* to the identity of all churches as the Church of God in faith, life and "agape." If in his own church the bishop is priest, teacher and pastor, the divinely appointed witness and keeper of the catholic faith, it is through the agreement of all bishops, as revealed in the synod, that all churches both manifest and maintain the ontological unity of Tradition, "For languages differ in the world, but the force of Tradition is the same" (St Irenaeus). The synod of bishops is not an organ of power over the Church, nor is it "greater" or "fuller" than the fullness of any local church, but in and through it all churches acknowledge and realize their ontological unity as the One, Holy, Catholic and Apostolic Church.

Ecclesiologically and dogmatically, the synod is *necessary* for the consecration of a bishop. The sacrament of order is its ecclesiological foundation[34] because, as we have seen, the synod is the essential condition of the fullness of each local church, of her "pleroma" as Body of Christ. But it also has another equally important function. The Church which by her very nature belongs to the new aeon, to the Kingdom of the age to come, abides yet in history, in time, in "this world." She is in *statu patriae*, but also in *statu viae*. She is Fullness, but she is also Mission, the Divine love, the Divine will of salvation addressed to the world. And it is by being Mission, by loving those for whom Christ died, that the Church realizes herself as the Fullness. A church that would isolate herself from the world and live by her eschatological fullness, that would cease to "evangelize," to bear witness to Christ in the world, would simply cease to be the Church—because the fullness by which she lives is

32 N. Zaozerskii, p. 223.
33 Cf. A. Khomiakov, "Letter to the Editor of L'Union Chrétienne" in *Complete Works* (in Russian) (1860) 2, pp. 30ff.
34 G. Florovsky, "The Sacrament of Pentecost (A Russian View on Apostolic Succession)" in *The Journal of the Fellowship of St Alban and St Sergius* 23 (March 1934) 29-34.

precisely the agape of God as revealed and communicated in Christ. "Mission" cannot, therefore, be a static relationship with the world. It means a fight with, and for, the world; it means a constant effort to understand and to challenge, to question and to answer. And this means finally that within the Church herself there must constantly arise doubts and problems and the need for a fresh renewal of the living testimony. The "world," both outside and inside the Church, tempts and challenges her with all its powers of destruction and doubt, idolatry and sin. This challenge calls for a common effort of all churches, for a faithful and living "koinonia" and agreement. It is this mission of the Church in the world, her "working" in time and history, that gives the synod its second function: to be the *common voice*, the common testimony of several (or all) churches in their ontological unity. Thus the apostolic synod meets not as a regular and necessary "organ" of the Church, but in connection with a problem arising out of the missionary situation in the Church. There is no evidence for any synod of this type until the end of the second century, when Montanism provoked a common resistance of the ecclesiastical body.[35] In the third century the African synod appears as a regular institution, but again its regularity is not that of an organ of power, but that of orderly consultations on common problems. Finally the Council of Nicaea and all subsequent Ecumenical Councils always convened to confront a problem which was vital to all churches and which required their common testimony. It is the *truth* of its decision and not any "constitutional right or guarantee" that makes it the highest authority in the Church.

VII

It is in the synod that *primacy* finds its first and most general expression. The synod, since its basic purpose is the consecration of a bishop, is primarily a *regional* synod, i.e., the council of a definite geographical area. The boundaries of such an area can be fixed in various ways: they can be geographical, or coincide with a political administrative unit or be the limits of Christian expansion from an ecclesiastical center: in church history there is ample evidence for all of these systems. But ecclesiastically the essential feature of a *district* is the participation of all its bishops in the

35   A Pokrovskii, *The Synods of the Early Church* (Sergiev Posad, 1914, in Russian).

consecration of a new bishop (cf. Canon 4 of Nicaea). And its second constitutive element is the existence among these bishops of a clearly defined primacy of the *first bishop*. This primacy is defined in the famous Apostolic Canon 34:

> The bishops of every nation must acknowledge him who is first among them and account him as their head, and do nothing of consequence without his consent…but neither let him (who is the first) do anything without the consent of all; for so there will be unanimity…

Here the essence of the regional primacy is stated quite clearly: it is not "power" or "jurisdiction" (for the primate can do nothing without the assent of all), but the expression of the unity and unanimity of all bishops and, consequently, of all churches of the area.

There is no need to go into all the details of the rather complicated history of the *metropolitan district* in the ancient church.[36] There can be little doubt that it was the most common, the most natural and basic form of relationship between local churches, the basic link of their unity, rooted in the sacrament of order. There can also be little doubt that for a long time the *local primacy* was universally understood and accepted as the basic expression of the very function of primacy. To use modern terminology, each "metropolitan district" was "autocephalous" (this is confirmed by Balsamon), since the main principle of "autocephaly" is precisely the right to elect and consecrate new bishops.

But local primacy is not the only form of primacy to be found in our canonical tradition. Almost from the very beginning there existed also wider groupings of churches with corresponding "centers of agreement" or primacy within them. One can argue which form of primacy appeared first. For, as it is well known, Christianity was settled first in the major cities of the Roman Empire and from there spread into the suburban areas. And since a metropolitan district implies the existence of a number of churches in a given area, it is only natural to think that at first the function of primacy belonged exclusively to the churches of the great metropolitan centers. Even after the growth in number of local churches and the consequent shaping of metropolitan districts, the original "centers" or "mother-churches" did not lose their special status, their particular primacy. One could call this later stage "second-degree primacy." In

36 V. Bolotov, *op. cit.*, vol. III.

the second and third centuries such was the position of Rome, Antioch, Alexandria, Lyons, Carthage, etc. What then were the nature and the functions of this form of primacy? The well-known Canon 6 of Nicaea applies to it the term *power* (*exousia*). But Bishop N. Milash in his commentary on this canon shows quite clearly that "power" here must be understood as "priority" or "privilege."[37] The canon defines the relationship between the Bishop of Alexandria and the four metropolitans of the Diocese of Egypt. In Egypt the metropolitan system appeared later than elsewhere and the Bishop of Alexandria, who was from the beginning the "head" of the whole Egyptian Church (i.e., the primate of all bishops), had, therefore, the privilege of primacy everywhere (i.e., the right to convene synods for the consecration of new bishops). The Council of Nicaea, which sanctioned the metropolitan system, had to establish for Egypt a kind of synthesis between the universal norm and the local particularities. On the one hand, it emphasized that no bishop could be consecrated without the assent of the metropolitan (thereby affirming "local primacy"), but, on the other hand, it left with the Bishop of Alexandria the ultimate approval of all elections. But, as a general rule, this latter form of primacy was defined in Nicaea as *priority*, and history shows clearly enough the nature of that priority: one can describe it as *primacy of authority*. Let us stress that we have here not so much the primacy of a bishop (as in the case of the metropolitan district), but the primacy of a particular church, her special spiritual and doctrinal authority among other churches. The great majority of local Christian communities were born from the missionary activity of some important urban church. From the latter they received the rule of faith, the rule of prayer and the "apostolic succession." Many of these great churches had, in addition, apostles or their first disciples for founders. Furthermore they were usually better equipped theologically and intellectually. It is natural, then, that in difficult or controversial cases, these churches took upon themselves the initiative of appeasement or, in other terms, of reaching and expressing the "agreement" of all churches. The local churches looked to them for guidance and counsel and recognized in their voice a special authority. We have early examples of such authority in the activity

37 N. Milash, v. I, pp. 194–204—To E. R. Hardy this canon indicates that the Bishop of Alexandria was *de facto* Metropolitan of the whole of Egypt; cf. *Christian Egypt: Church and People* (New York, 1952), pp. 54–9.

of St Ignatius of Antioch, St Polycarp of Smyrna, St Irenaeus of Lyons, and later, in the councils of Antioch and Carthage. Yet primacy of authority here cannot be defined in juridical terms, because it has nothing to do with "*jus*" as such; yet it was quite real in the life of the early church, and the seeds of the future patriarchates are to be found in it. Once again, we must stress that its essence and purpose is not "power," but manifestation of the existent unity of the churches in faith and life.

Finally we come to the highest and ultimate form of primacy: *universal primacy*. An age-long anti-Roman prejudice has led some Orthodox canonists simply to deny the existence of such primacy in the past or the need for it in the present. But an objective study of the canonical tradition cannot fail to establish beyond any doubt that, along with local "centers of agreement" or primacies, the Church had also known a universal primacy. The ecclesiological error of Rome lies not in the affirmation of her universal primacy. Rather, the error lies in her identification of this primacy with "supreme power," which transforms Rome into the *principium radix et origio*[38] of the unity of the Church and of the Church herself. This ecclesiological distortion, however, must not force us into a simple rejection of universal primacy. On the contrary, it ought to encourage its genuinely Orthodox interpretation.

It is impossible to deny that, even before the appearance of local primacies, the Church from the first days of her existence possessed an ecumenical center of unity and agreement. In the apostolic and the Judaeo-Christian period, it was the Church of Jerusalem, and later the Church of Rome—"presiding in *agape*," according to St Ignatius of Antioch. This formula and the definition of the universal primacy contained in it have been aptly analyzed by Fr Afanassieff and we need not repeat his argument here.[39] Neither can we quote here all the testimonies of the fathers and the councils unanimously acknowledging Rome as the senior church and the center of ecumenical agreement.[40] It is only for the sake of biased polemics that one can ignore these testimonies, their

38 "Encycl. S. Offic. *Ad Episcopos Angliae*, 16 Sept., 1864," in *Denzinger Banwart*, ed., 10, no. 1686.
39 "The Catholic Church," in *Pravoslavnaia Mysl'* 11.
40 Much evidence, though analyzed from a Roman Catholic point of view, has been gathered by P. Batiffol, *L'Eglise Naissante et le Catholicisme* (Paris, 1927)—*La Paix Constantinienne* (Paris, 1929)—*Le Siège Apostolique* (Paris, 1924)—*Cathedra Petri* (Paris, 1938).

consensus and significance. It has happened, however, that if Roman historians and theologians have always interpreted this evidence in *juridical* terms, thus falsifying its real meaning, their Orthodox opponents have systematically belittled the evidence itself. Orthodox theology is still awaiting a truly Orthodox evaluation of universal primacy in the first millennium of church history—an evaluation free from polemical or apologetic exaggerations. Such study will certainly reveal that the essence and purpose of this primacy is to express and preserve the unity of the Church in faith and life; to express and preserve the unanimity of all churches; to keep them from isolating themselves into ecclesiastical provincialism, loosing the catholic ties, separating themselves from the unity of life. It means ultimately to assume the care, the *sollicitudo*,[41] of the churches so that each one of them can abide in that fullness which is always the *whole* catholic tradition and not any "part" of it.

From this brief analysis of the concept of primacy we can draw the following general conclusion: primacy in the Church is not "supreme power," this notion being incompatible with the nature of the Church as Body of Christ. But neither is primacy a mere "chairmanship" if one understands this term in its modern, parliamentary and democratic connotations. It has its roots, as all other functions, in the Church—Body of Christ. In each church there fully abides and is always "actualized" the Church of God; yet all together the churches are still the same one and indivisible Church of God, the Body of Christ. The Church of God is manifested in the plurality of the churches; but because ontologically they are the *same* Church, this ontological identity is expressed in a visible, living, and constantly renewed link: the unity of faith, the unity of action and mission, the common care for everything that constitutes the task of Church in *statu viae*. A local church cannot isolate herself, become a center in herself, live "by herself" and by her own local and private interests, because the *fullness* which constitutes her very being is precisely the fullness of the catholic faith and catholic mission, the fullness of Christ who fills all things in all. The Church cannot realize

---

41 It is noteworthy that after having analyzed all early Christian evidence on the primacy of Rome, Batiffol reaches an almost identical conclusion—"The papacy of the first centuries is the authority exercised by the Church of Rome among other churches, authority which consists in caring after their conformity with the authentic tradition of faith...and which is claimed by no other church but the Church of Rome"—*Cathedra Petri*, p. 28.

this fullness, make it her own, and, therefore, be the Church, without *ipso facto* living in all and by all; and this means living in the universal conscience of the Church "scattered in the whole world and yet abiding as if it were in one home." A local church cut off from this universal "koinonia" is indeed a *contradictio in adjecto*, for this koinonia is the very essence of the Church. And it has, therefore, its *form* and *expression:* primacy. Primacy is the necessary expression of the unity in faith and life of all local churches, of their living and efficient koinonia.

Now we can return to our first definition of primacy. Primacy *is* power, but as power it is not different from the power of a bishop in each church. It is not a *higher power* but indeed the same power, only expressed, manifested, realized by one. The primate *can* speak for all because the Church is one and because the power he exercises is the power of each bishop and of all bishops. And he *must* speak for all because this very unity and agreement require, in order to be efficient, a special organ of expression, a mouth, a voice. Primacy is thus a necessity because therein is the expression and manifestation of the unity of the churches as being the unity of *the* Church. And it is important to remember that the primate, as we know him from our canonical tradition, is always the bishop of a local church and not a "bishop at large," and that primacy belongs to him precisely because of his status in his own church.[42] It is not a personal charism, but rather a function of the whole Church, carried and fulfilled by its bishop. The early tradition clearly indicates the primacy of the Church of Rome, yet we know next to nothing about the first bishops of Rome, who, evidently, served as ministers of this primacy. The idea of primacy thus excludes the idea of jurisdictional power but implies that of an "order" of churches which does not subordinate one church to another, but which makes it possible for all churches to live together this life of all in each and of each in all, thereby fulfilling the mystery of the Body of Christ, the fullness "filling all in all."

VIII

This concept of primacy, as has been said already, is rooted in the "eucharistic ecclesiology" which we believe to be the source of the

42 Cf. G. Florovsky, *The Sacrament of Pentecost*, p. 31.

Orthodox canonical and liturgical tradition. As a result of its distortion or, at least, "metamorphosis," there appeared another type of ecclesiology which we have termed "universal." It leads necessarily to the understanding and practice of primacy as "supreme power" and, therefore, to a *universal bishop* as source and foundation of jurisdiction in the whole ecclesiastical structure. The Orthodox Church has condemned this distortion in its pure and explicit Roman Catholic form. This does not mean, however, that our church life is free from its poison. Universal ecclesiology is a permanent temptation because in the last analysis it is a *natural* one, being the product of a "naturalization" of Christianity, its adaptation to the life "after the rudiments of the world, and not after Christ." Only the historical sources of this temptation in the East are different from those in the West. And inasmuch as all the controversies within Orthodoxy are obviously centered on this basic question of the nature of the Church, we must conclude this article with a short analysis of our own deficiencies.

At a relatively recent date there arose among the Orthodox the opinion that the Church is based in her life on the principle of autocephaly, the term "autocephalous" here being applied exclusively to the Eastern patriarchates or the great national churches. According to this opinion, the principle of autocephaly is not only one of the historical "expressions" by the Church of her universal structure, but precisely *the* ecclesiological foundation of the Church and her life. In other words, the unique universal organism of Roman ecclesiology is opposed here to "autocephalous" organisms, each one constituted by several "dioceses" under one center of "supreme power." All these "autocephalies" are absolutely equal among themselves, and this equality exclude any universal center or primacy.[43]

The appearance of this theory and its almost unanimous acceptance by contemporary Orthodox canonists is very significant. In the first place, the principle of autocephaly has indeed been for the last few

---

43 The most "theological" expression of this theory is to be found in the articles, mentioned above, of the Hieromonk Sophrony and E. Kovalevsky. In a more juridical way it is defended by S. V. Troitsky; Cf. J. Meyendorff, "Constantinople and Moscow," in *Tserkovnyi Vestnik* 15, pp. 5–9. Finally its justification in terms of ecclesiastical nationalism is given by M. Polskii, *The Canonical Status of the Supreme Ecclesiastical Government* (Jordanville, 1948); cf. my essay "The Church and Ecclesiastical Structure" (Paris, 1949).

centuries the unique principle of organization in Orthodoxy and, therefore, its "acting" canonical rule. The reason is clear: "autocephaly" with this particular meaning is fully adequate to the specifically Eastern form of Christian "nationalism," or reduction of the Church to the "natural world." This explains in turn why of all possible forms it was precisely "autocephaly" which became for centuries the "acting canon law" in the Eastern Church and today is accepted by so many as an eternal and unchangeable principle of her canonical tradition.

All the deficiencies in the ecclesiological conscience in the East can be ascribed to two major sources: the close "identification" of the Church with the state (Byzantine "symphony" and its varieties), and religious nationalism. Both explain the unchallenged triumph of the theory of "autocephaly."

The identification of the Church with the state (cf. the confused and often tragic history of Byzantine theocracy) deeply changed the very notion of *power* in the Church. It was shaped more and more after the "juridical" pattern of the state, and its understanding as a charismatic ministry within the Body of Christ was consequently weakened. More precisely, there occurred a rupture between sacramental and jurisdictional power. A bishop, to receive his power, was, of course, still to be consecrated. Yet in fact the source of his "jurisdictional power" rested now with a "supreme power," before which he was to become "responsible." The bishop's "report" to the synod offers the best example of this change, as it indicates first the quick transformation of the function of the synod in Byzantium, and second the equally rapid growth of a real "mystique" of the supreme power in the person of the patriarch.

We know that in the early church the synod was by its very nature a gathering of bishops (i.e., a more or less regular convention and not a permanent institution). There were regular or extraordinary synods, but in all of them the essential condition of their very "function" was the living identity of each bishop and his church—for it was only as "head" of his church, its *proistamenos* in the deepest sense of this word, that he took part in the synod, which thus became the *expression* of the unity and the unanimity of the churches as the Churches of God. Beginning with the fourth century, although not everywhere at the same time, this idea of the synod was progressively replaced by another one: as the supreme and central power *over* the churches. The best example here is the famous

synodos endemousa in Constantinople, which became the pattern for the
future "synod." Brought into existence at first as a synod *ad hoc*—an
occasional meeting of bishops who happened to be in Constantinople—
this synod became little by little a permanent organ of power assisting the
patriarch,[44] with the result that the condition for participation in it was
reversed: a bishop left his church in order to become a member of this
governing body. The bishops became, so to speak, "power in themselves," and their synod became the supreme or central power. One step
more, from the jurisdictional point of view, and the bishops have become representatives or delegates of this high power even in their own
churches. This is, of course, only a scheme, but it would not be difficult
to substantiate it with facts.[45] The road from the *synodos endemousa* to
the "Governing Synod" of the Russian Church is a straight one, complicated, it is true, by influences of the Western and Protestant "synodal"
law...Yet the source of both is in the state, in its notion of "supreme
power" as source of any "local power."

Not less characteristic is the development of what may be termed
"patriarchal mystique," which finds its first expression in the development of the power of the Patriarch of Constantinople. In its essence this
mystique is radically different from that of the Pope. The latter has its
roots in the experience of the Church as a universal organism, called to
dominate the world; the former in the parallelism between church and
empire which required an ecclesiastical "counterpart" of the *basileus*.
Although one must stress again and again that the origin of the Byzantine patriarch's power is not "lust of power" but the "Byzantine analogy"
between the two supreme powers,[46] yet here also it is the state and not
the church that shapes this new idea of power.

The metamorphosis of the very concept of "power," its disconnec-
tion, even if partial, from the ecclesiology of the Body of Christ and, as
the natural result, the emergence of a "supreme power"—all this consti-

44 M. Skaballanovich, *The Byzantine State and the Church in the 11th Century* (St Petersburg,
    1884, in Russian); E. Gerland, "Die Vorgeschichte des Patriarchats des Kpl.," in *Byz. Neues
    Jahrb.* IX, 218.
45 I. Sokolov, "The Election of Bishops in Byzantium" in *Vizantiiskii Vremennik* 22 (1915-16)
    (in Russian).
46 Cf. my essays, "The Destiny of Byzantine Theocracy" in *Pravoslavnaia Mysl'* 6 (in Russian)
    and "Byzantine Theocracy and the Orthodox Church," in *St Vladimir's Seminary Quarterly*
    (1953).

tutes the first and yet most tragic crisis in the history of Orthodox ecclesiology. The time has come, it seems to us, to admit openly that the Byzantine period of our history, which in many respects is still for us the golden age of Orthodoxy, saw, nevertheless, the beginning of an ecclesiological disease. The mystique of the "symphonia" (with its only alternative being the monastic "desert" and the individual work for "salvation") obscured the reality of the Church as People of God, as the Church of God and the Body of Christ manifested and edified in every place. It was the triumph of universal ecclesiology in its Byzantine form.

The state and its idea of power are, however, but the first of the two major causes of that disease. The second, not less important in its consequences, was the growth of *religious nationalism*. No one, I think, will deny that one of the fruits of Byzantine theocracy, which for a long time obscured the life of the Orthodox East, was the growth of those religious nationalisms which little by little identified the Church, her structure and organization, with the *nation*, making her the religious expression of national existence. This national existence, however natural and therefore legitimate it may be, is by its every essence a "partial" existence—the existence as a "part"' of humanity which, though not necessarily inimical to its other "parts," is nonetheless opposed to them as "one's own" to the "alien." The early church knew herself to be the *tertium genus*, in which there is neither Greek nor Jew. This means that it proclaimed and conveyed a Life which, without rejecting the "partial" and natural life, could transform it into "wholeness" or *catholicity*. Hence it must be clear that religious nationalism is essentially a heresy about the Church, for it reduces grace and the new life to "nature" and makes the latter a formal principle of the Church's structure. This does not mean that there can be no Christian people or any Christian vocation of a nation; it means only that a Christian nation (i.e., a nation which has acknowledged its Christian vocation) does not *become* the Church. Because the nature of the Church is the Body of Christ, she belongs to the Kingdom of the age to come and cannot identify herself with anything in "this world..."

Yet it is precisely this religious nationalism in combination with the new "statelike" concept of power which supplied the basis for the new theory of autocephaly and made it for centuries the "acting canon law" in the Orthodox East. I have tried to show elsewhere the weak points in contemporary attempts to justify this theory and to erect it into an ecclesiological absolute. From the point of view which interests us here, however, the negative significance of this theory (defended, on the one hand, as justification of the national divisions of Orthodoxy and, on the other, as sanction for the prevalent administrative centralism) introduces into the Orthodox doctrine of the Church the very elements of "universal ecclesiology" which she rejects and condemns as it is. It obscures the sacramental structure of the Church rooted in its life as Body of Christ, by a "national" structure, thus making a natural organism.

On the essential falsehood of this theory and on its fateful consequences in the life of the Church much has been written. One can affirm that the ecclesiastical consciousness has never "received" it as Tradition—as witness about the nature of the Church. Neither the doctrine of the "five senses," which was the first reaction of Byzantine canonists to Roman claims, nor the absolute "autocephalism" of national theocracies, born as it was out of the fight against the theocracy of Byzantium, nor the synodal regime of the Russian Church—none of these succeeded in being accepted as an organic expression of church consciousness or in obscuring to the end the genuine and living sources of ecclesiastical life. This source is still in the true canonical tradition and in the sacraments by which the Church lives and realizes herself...

Is it necessary to mention all the harm done to the Church by this acting "canon law," disconnected as it is from the living sources of Orthodox ecclesiology? Such as, on the one hand, the bureaucratic spirit pervading the Church, making her the "religious department"; the absence of a living "sobornost"; the transformation of dioceses into mere administrative units living under the control of abstract "centers"; the abyss between the "power" and the body of the Church and, as the result of this, the "revolt of the masses"; the introduction into the Church of the ideas of "representation of interests" of this or that category, be it of "lay control" or of division between clergy and laity, etc....Or, on the other hand, the deep and tragic division of Orthodoxy into national churches, each indifferent to the other, living in and by itself, the crisis of the universal consciousness, and the weakening of the catholic links...

We must hope, however, that this crisis is not a mortal one. The strength of Christ is fulfilled in weakness and the gates of hell cannot prevail against the Church. In sufferings and sorrows there appears today a new thirst for the *truth* about the Church, a new interest in discovering the genuine sources of her life. The question which we raised and attempted to answer, however partially and schematically, in this article, that of "primacy," cannot be separated from a deep and consistent return to Orthodox ecclesiology.

Contributors

Nicholas Afanasieff (d. 1966) was a professor of canon law and church history at the Orthodox Theological Institute in Paris. His numerous studies, published mainly in Russian and French, include *Trapeza Gospodnya* ("The Table of the Lord") (Paris, 1955), *Sluzhenie miryan v tserkvi* ("The Ministry of the Laity in the Church") (Paris, 1955) and *L'Église du Saint-Esprit* (Paris, 1975).

Nicholas Koulomzine is a professor of New Testament at the Orthodox Theological Institute in Paris, and the author of a study on "The Son of Man."

Veselin Kesich is Professor Emeritus of New Testament at St Vladimir's Orthodox Theological Seminary, Crestwood, New York, and the author of *The Gospel Image of Christ* (St Vladimir's Seminary Press, 1992), *The First Day of the New Creation* (St Vladimir's Seminary Press, 1981), and other studies.

John Meyendorff is dean and professor of church history and patristics at St Vladimir's Seminary. Among his numerous publications are *A Study of Gregory Palamas* (second English edition, 1974); *Christ in Eastern Christian Thought* (Corpus Books, 1969, repr. St Vladimir's Seminary Press, 1975); *Byzantine Theology. Historical Trends and Doctrinal Themes* (Fordham University Press, 1974); *Byzantium and the Rise of Russia* (Cambridge University Press, 1981; repr. paper, St Vladimir's Seminary Press, 1989); *Imperial Unity and Christian Divisions. The Church, 450-680 AD* (St Vladimir's Seminary Press, 1989).

Alexander Schmemann (d. 1983) was dean of St Vladimir's Seminary (1962-83) and taught church history and liturgical theology. He is the author of *An Introduction to Liturgical Theology* (1986), *For the Life of the World* (1970), *Of Water and the Spirit* (1974), and other books.

Index

Index of Biblical References